I0414384

GENERAL STUDIES
IN EDUCATION

POLITICAL ECONOMY
SCIENCE AND TECHNOLOGY
IN SOCIETY

By

KAYODE ASOGA – ALLEN

SECOND EDITION

First published 2003

ISBN 978-1535240369

www.kayodeasogaallen.com

DEDICATION

This book is dedicated to late Chief Moshood Kasimawo Olawale Abiola for sacrificing his life for the enthronement of democracy in Nigeria and for his philanthropic gestures to sports, education and other national sectors during his life time. His charitable work and indeed his concerns and assistance to the poor would long be remembered.

PREFACE

This book has been written for students in tertiary institutions to cater for their academic needs in Political Economy and Science and Technology in Society which are courses offered under the General Studies Programme.

This book would furnish the users with sufficient background knowledge that would make them stars in answering questions relating to the fields. Most of the examples are based on the issues in Nigeria, Africa and the world in general.

I hereby congratulate the Nigerian students and the general public on the emergence of additional knowledge in the field of General Studies in Education. Wishing you all, success as you study hard and make use of facts contained in this book.

Kayode Asoga-Allen
B.A. Ed. (History) Ogun.
M.Ed (Curriculum/Social Studies) Ibadan.
PhD in view

ACKNOWLEDGEMENT

First and foremost, I wish to express my unconditional gratitude to Almighty God, the owner of wisdom and author of life for enriching and endowing me with knowledge that is beneficial to people. It is neither by power nor by might, but by the spirit of Jehovah.

I wish to thank the following people for their innumerable contributions towards the success of this book whether directly or indirectly. They are Dr. Osokoya, I. O.; Head of Department of Teacher Education, University of Ibadan. Mr. Adenuga A. O., Head of Department of Political Science, Tai Solarin College of Education, Ijebu-Ode. Dr. (Mrs.) Ojetunde, C. F., Mr. Unoroh S. O., both of the Department of English, School of Languages, MOCPED. Mr. Adeleye A. A., teacher of English at Tomia Community Secondary School, Alagbado, Lagos.

I wish to show special appreciation to my Provost Prince Ekemode, K. O. for his constructive critcism of the manuscript. Indeed, his thoroughness and his insistence on scholastic work has added value to the quality of this book.

My gratitude also goes to my loving wife Rebecca Oluyemisi and my children Ademola, Adeola, Adedoyin and Adeyinka for their understanding, encouragement and cooperation.

Lastly, I wish to thank all my colleagues and Senior colleagues in all schools and departments of MOCPED. God bless you all.

Table of Contents

Chapter One: Political Economy

1.1 The Concept of "Political" in Political Economy

The word "political" is connected with government or public affairs of a country and its relations with other countries. To hold political power is to be in charge of affairs of a people, and the nation in general.

People seek political power to be able to manage the affairs of other people, be it at the local, state or federal level. Political power can be acquired in the following ways:

1. **Through political** party: That is by belonging to a political party through which one contests and wins an election.

2. **Through the use of force: (coup de tat")**: as found in the military when the military seizes power from democratically elected government and start to direct the affairs of a nation and its people, we say that political power is in the hands of the military. In modern days, it is generally accepted that military government is an aberration and uncalled for in any nation. Democracy is the order of the day in developed nations and the wind of democracy is fast blowing across developing nations of the world. However, whether it is military or democratically

elected government, the issue at stake is political power.

3.   **By Nomination**: One may be nominated to hold political office. This is done both in military or democratic government. The only difference is that in the military, the president can solely or single-handedly appoint people to political offices without any interference or criticism from any quarter, but in democracy, the executive president nominates and sends names of nominees to the legislators or the legislative house for approval. The legislature would now invite the nominees for screening. If any of the nominees is found unworthy in character to hold political office perhaps, as a result of his bad records or his past activities, he could be disqualified by the legislators. To acquire political power in a democratic society, people engage in politics. Politics is the game of power. It is an act of wooing others with good promises (manifesto) in order to gain their mandate to serve them. Those who engage in politics are called politicians. However, man is a political animal. Man participates in politics directly or indirectly, in essence, no man is completely out of politics.

1.2   The Concept of "Economy" in Political Economy

Economy can be defined in various ways: for example, it

can be defined as the system by which a country's money and goods are produced; or the means by which a country produces wealth and acquire those things it cannot produce. Economy can also be defined as the careful use of money, time, goods etc., so that nothing is wasted. One can also define economy as something that is done in order to spend less money. It is the means by which a country derives its income, because a country derives its income through production of goods and services. No country is self-sufficient in as much as it cannot produce all that it needs.

A country produces in surplus quantity the goods in which she has comparative advantage over others and exchanges them with other nations or countries that produce in large quantity what she cannot produce. That is the essence of international trade. When we talk of a country's economic resources, we mean the various sources by which a country derives her income. For example, the economic resources of Nigeria include crude oil, timber, cocoa, coal, bitumen, groundnut, palm oil, gas to mention a few. The economic prosperity of a nation depends largely on the available resources in that nation and the ability to tap and utilize these resources as well as the effective and efficient management of income accruing to the country.

1.3   The Concept of Political Economy

Political economy can be defined as the political and economic studies of a nation in terms of ways by which political decisions affect the economy. Basically, of all the factors that play prominent role in human society, economic factor is paramount. Economic needs are basic human needs and unless man is able to meet these needs he may not survive. Political factor essentially controls all other factors. He that possesses political power controls the economic, religious and social factors. For instance, the president of a country takes decisions or initiates economic policies for the nation. In Nigeria, the former democratic government of President Olusegun Obasanjo took some economic decisions that had effects on the nation. Such decisions include banning of second hand fridges/refrigerators, second hand cars that are more than eight years old, frozen foods e.g. turkey, chicken and so on and so forth.

Political Economy can also be defined as the study of how politics affects the economy in terms of economic system adopted and being adopted by the past and present governments of a country and the extent to which the system is beneficial or detrimental to the welfare of the masses. Political economy brings to the limelight the negative or positive impacts, on a nation or the people and government in general, of an economic system adopted by the government.

As far as Nigeria is concerned, the various economic systems adopted prior to pre and post-independence include feudalism, capitalism and welfarism. The magnitude of the involvement in each of the systems would be discussed. Also the various economic policies adopted by the government during the economic depression of 1980s and 1990s includes Structural Adjustment Programme (SAP), Austerity Measure (AM), devaluation of currency, removal of subsidy on feeding of Nigerian students in tertiary institutions, removal of subsidy on petroleum products, retrenchment of workers, negotiation for foreign loans. Most of these measures were dictated to the government of Nigeria by World Bank and International Monetary Fund (IMF). Most of these policies yielded little or no positive result, they only added to the suffering of the masses.

Reduction in government spending only affected the welfare programmes such as free education, bursary award to students of tertiary institutions, subsidy on electricity, health, transportation etc. which people hitherto enjoyed.

1.4   Rationale for Studying Political Economy

Before a course is incorporated into the curriculum of any programme there must be some specific objectives which the course is designed to achieve. Political Economy, as a course in teacher education curriculum, is not an exemption. The rationale for the course includes:

i.   To produce teachers who are conversant with the economic systems operated and being operated in their country.

ii. The teacher has two important resources to manage; these are human and material resources. Knowledge of Political Economy would help in making the prospective teacher a prudent and efficient manager of these resources.

iii. The system of education a nation adopts depends largely on the economic resources available to the nation, thus, teachers should possess a sound knowledge of the relationship between education and economy.

iv. The knowledge of Political Economy exposes teachers to the various world economic systems vis-a-vis their strengths and shortcomings.

v.   Political Economy provides the teachers with the pre-requisite knowledge needed to participate in any national debate on the economic system best suited for the nation

vi. The knowledge of Political Economy would enable the teachers to play advisory roles to the government on economic matters.

vii. It acquaints teachers with detailed historical background of the economic system being operated, so as to be able to trace the reasons for economic problems being faced by the nation.

viii. Teachers, being manpower trainers, must be able to discuss issues relating to the economy. Knowledge of Political Economy would undoubtedly help teachers to perform this role more effectively and efficiently.

ix.   Political Economy acquaints teachers with the knowledge of the culture as well as the arts and crafts of the people of the country.

x.   It furnishes the teacher with the requisite knowledge of the relationship between political and economic factors as both go hand in hand in human society.

xi.   It enables the teachers to appraise the economic achievements of a particular government.

1.5   Revision Questions

a.   Explain the concept of "Political" in Political Economy

b.   Explain the concept of "Economy" in Political Economy

c.   Give a clear definition of Political Economy

d.   Justify the inclusion of Political Economy in the curriculum of Teacher Education

Chapter Two: World Economic Systems

2.1 Feudalism

Feudalism is an economic and administrative system based on the principle of land ownership. In the ancient days prior to the evolution of modern governmental systems, feudalism was practised in Nigeria. The owners of land were Kings and Emirs. In the pre-colonial period there were powerful Emirs and Kings who established their hegemony over territories and made their subjects to pay something to the Royal treasury for the land they occupied.

The King/Emir appointed middlemen called tenant-in-chiefs and lent the land to them. The tenant-in-chiefs were the only people known to the Emirs/Kings, and they were the lords over the land. The tenant-in-chiefs in turn sublet the land to another group of people over whom they had authority under the following conditions:

i. They had to contribute soldiers to support the lords whenever there was any war.

ii. They had to support the lords financially by paying something to the royal treasury. This may be in cash and kind.

iii. They had to pledge their absolute loyalty to the lords

The payment made by this tenant is known as "fee" it is from the "fee" that the word "feudalism" is derived.

Feudalism is an ancient economic system and it is rarely practised nowadays. However, it is still being practised in the rural parts of Western Nigeria.

2.2   Feudalism in Northern/Western Nigeria

The way feudalism was practised in Northern part of Nigeria is different from the way it was practised in the Yoruba land of Western Nigeria. For instance, in Northern Nigeria all the inhabitants of an emirate were all tenants of the Emir and were made to pay fees to him for the land they occupied. But in Yoruba land, only the people of the conquered territories, town or villages and those who left their homeland to settle in the area were treated as tenants, and had to pay fees to the king. Even in some cases not only the king owns tenants, some chiefs and heads of families also have tenants from whom they collected fees. It was compulsory for any stranger who moved to settle in Yorubaland of old to farm to be under a lord who ensured his protection from unnecessary harassment of the other indigenes.

2.3 Advantages of Feudalism

i. The system provided poor people with means of livelihood as they were given land to farm on. An adage says when food is out of poverty, poverty is minimized or reduced.

ii. The poor people were protected from aggression or unnecessary harassment of the indigenes who might wish to exploit them.

iii. The system guaranteed absolute loyalty of the tenants to the lords

iv. The Kings/Emirs and the lords were adequately protected

v. The Kings/Emirs derived income from the system.

vi. It enhanced the authority of the King/Emirs on their territories and made them more powerful.

vii. There was no form of opposition from the tenants

2.4 Disadvantages of Feudalism

i. People were deprived of their fundamental human rights as they were not permitted to have a say in matter affecting them.

ii. The system concentrated too much power in the hands of the Emirs/Kings and too much power in an individual's hands is prone to being abused. Power corrupts, absolute power corrupts absolutely.

iii. The tenants were treated like slaves in their country.

iv. The Kings/Emirs and lords were more interested in the security and safety of themselves and their families than about the safety of the tenants and their families.

v. The system tended to make people tenants in the land given to them by God.

vi. It is an ancient system that is no more useful in the modern time.

vii. If the land is not productive the tenants may be at a colossal loss.

2.5   Capitalism

Capitalism is an economic system based on private ownership of means of production and distribution of goods and services. That is, private individual (capitalist) determines what to produce, the means of producing it in terms of capital requirement, the price of the goods produced vis-a-vis the distribution strategies. Unlike the situation with welfarism or socialism where the government fixes prices of goods produced by the state; in capitalism, prices are determined only by the capitalist. In essence, the government of the state has little or no control over the goods and their prices in a capitalist economy.

Capitalism as an economic system is being practised by countries like the United States of America, Germany, France, Britain etc. Capitalism places great emphasis on individual's ability to maximise the means of acquiring more capital and hence makes him highly industrious.

2.6   The Genesis of Capitalism in Nigeria

The origin of capitalism in Nigeria could be traced back to the colonial days.   During the Industrial Revolution in Europe, there was great demand for Nigerian raw materials for European industries.   This development brought about export and import between Nigeria and Europe.   To this end, the colonialists set up marketing board charged with the responsibility of determining the worth of Nigerian agricultural produce.   The marketing boards were used by the colonialists as a means of appropriation and exploitation.   The peasant farmers were paid less than the actual value of their goods.   This enabled the Europeans to get cheap raw materials for their industries and the finished products sold back to the people at exorbitant prices.   This exploitation helped to impoverish the country while it helped to develop the

European economy.

After Nigeria obtained her political independence, the Nigerians that succeeded the colonialists continued to follow the footstep of the colonial masters. They started to exploit their people. Thus, this class of Nigerians became the bourgeoisies. They became very wealthy, with their wealth being made at the expense of the majority who wallow in abject poverty. Most of this group of Nigerians today dominate the political class. They have surplus money to build estate for themselves, send their children to the best universities abroad and finance political parties. That is the reasons why there is a wide gap existing between the rich and the poor in the country. These capitalists control the economy and politics of the nation because of their wealth.

2.7   Advantages of Capitalism

Capitalism as an economic system has the following advantages:

i.   Capitalism allows individual capitalist to make profit. Every person or group of persons investing often does so with the motive of making profit.

ii.   The individual capitalist enjoys the monopoly of fixing prices for their produce or goods without any interference.

iii.   Capitalism gives room for specialization of labour. Each skilled worker knows what he is to do in the process of production and concentrates on that specific aspect.

iv.   Capitalism encourages competition among the capitalists in the production of goods. This does not only enhance the quality of goods and services at low prices but also lead to improvement in the standard of living.

v.   Capitalism encourages an enterprising spirit and makes people eager to do something.

vi.   It helps to increase the Gross Domestic Product (GDP) as well as the national income.

vii.   It breaks the government monopoly of being the sole provider of goods and services in the state.

2.8   Disadvantages of Capitalism

i.   Job prospects of the workers is determined by the proprietor as well as workers' salaries. In any event of economic depression, workers may be thrown out

ii.   Capitalism tends to make only few people rich while the majority wallow in poverty and penury.

iii.   Competition in capitalism, though advantageous, is detrimental to small scale industries' prosperity. This is because the capitalist may wish to exploit all the available trade opportunities and this would force the small scale industries to liquidate. For example, a situation whereby a fuel station sells kerosene in bottles apart from selling in gallons can make those who buy in small quantities to fold up.

iv. Capitalism deprives human beings from using their initiative because the division of labour or specialization allows the worker to perform only one role in the process of production. As a matter of fact much of work of individual has been taken over by the machine.

v. The monopoly of fixing the prices of goods by the individual capitalist may be abused thereby leading to exorbitant prices.

vi. It makes the government less effective in determining what is to be produced and how to produce it as well as prices of goods

vii. In a capitalist economy, wealthy and powerful capitalists may hijack the power of the authority in the state by influencing only the policies that can benefit them alone rather than mass oriented policies.

viii. It places the economic well-being of the majority in the hands of few people or minority.

ix. It is capable of causing economic inequality in the society whereby some people live a quality and standard life because of abundant resources at their disposal while others manage to survive.

2.9   Socialism

This is an economic system in which the public owns and controls the means of production, land, capital and labour and even their allocation among the people in the society.   Morrison's view, cited by Appadorai (1975) defined socialism as "a theory and a movement aiming at the collective organization of the community in the interest of the masses through the common ownership and collective control of the means of production and exchange.   Its essentials are that all great industries and the land should be publicly and collectively owned and that, they should be conducted in conformity with a national economic plan for the common good instead of for private benefits"

Arokodare (1995), citing the view of a socialist, A. C. Pigous, points out that socialism tends to abolish all forms of private control of means of production and profit making and replace this with common ownership of property and control planning of social good.   The view of the socialists in the process of achieving the above objective differs from one another.   Some opined that to achieve a true socialist society,   there   must   be   "revolution"   through   the dictatorship of the proletariat (the workers) and monopoly of power by the communist parties. The communists and syndicalists belong to this school of thought exemplified by the Russia Socialist Revolution of 1917. On the other hand, another school of thought (the collectivists and the guild socialists) members of the British Labour Party, the French, American, Canada, socialist parties, and the German and Scandinavian Social Democratic parties believe that socialist society is attainable by evolution i.e. through democratic and peaceful means such as organization of the socialist parties, their victory on election, and resultant control of government with socialist policies.

According to Appadorai (1975) the essentials of socialist economy are as follow:

i.   The exaltation of the community above individual;

ii.   The equalization of human conditions;

iii.   The elimination of the capitalists;

iv.   The expropriation of the landlords;

v.   The extinction of the private enterprise; and

vi.   The eradication of competition

Discussion on socialism will be incomplete without briefly describing the essential principles of communism as contained in the Communist Manifesto of Karl Marx (the father of socialism) issued in 1848.

These include:

i. **The materialistic interpretation of history**: According to Karl Marx, it is the material or economic condition of a society that actually forms the bedrock on which the others shares e.g. political, social, religious etc. The economic relation is termed the 'substructure' while others are superstructure.

ii. **The class struggle or war**: This refers to the rivalry that occurs between the two classes of either feudal or capitalist society. For instance, the workers suffer a lot and get little in return in their productive activities in a capitalist system while their employers reap the accruing resources. This cause war.

iii. **The theory of surplus value**: This manifests in the surplus labour being rendered by the workers in a class-oriented society. The workers work much but get little thus, creating surplus value for the benefit of the capitalist.

iv. **A social revolution**: Since the capitalist interest is mainly on accumulating wealth at the expense of the workers, the latter become wiser and organize themselves into a formidable social group so as to overthrow the capitalist from power.

v. **The dictatorship of the proletariat**: The dominated class (the workers) relentlessly struggle to eliminate the few exploiters from power, confiscate means of production from them, organise labour, and establish state factories and so on. This is a path towards achieving a classless society

vi. **The withering away of the unjust state**: After destruction of capitalism, the state will wither away and a new social order emerges

vii. The principle of "from each according to his capacity and to each according to his need" will become the central operational principle in the new social order, which is the socialist economy. Everybody will be obliged to contribute his quota to the development of the society, while the states too strive to meet individual needs accordingly.

2.10 Advantages of Socialism

The advantages of socialism are as follow:

i. The state determines the economic activities in terms of what to produce, the means of production, and the price of the goods produced, as against individual's determination of prices in capitalism.

ii. It disallows monopolistic control of the national economy by the rich few.

iii. It removes all sorts of evils or ills associated

with market price mechanisms because a central body controls the prices of goods.

iv. It ensures job security for workers because the wages of workers are paid by the government.

v. It eliminates all sorts of wastages associated with capitalism where over-production often occurs as a result of competition, because the government controls production.

vi. In socialism, there are labour laws that guide the activities of both the workers and the relevant authorities.

vii. It gives room for equitable distribution of national resources and ensures the same standard of living for the people.

viii. It disallows exploitation of the masses, since the aim is not to make profit but to cater for the masses.

2.11   Disadvantages of Socialism

Rarely is there anything that has advantages without having disadvantages.   Among other things, the following are the disadvantages of socialism as an economic system:

i. Government monopolises decision on what to produce, how to produce and how to distribute it.

ii. The workers or producers are not allowed to use

their initiative in the production and distribution process except as dictated by the central body.

iii. Long bureaucratic process may hamper quick decisions thereby resulting in undue delays. More-so as government has to approve all economic policies before they are implemented.

iv. A change of government in a socialist state can affect production; this is because different governments have different ideologies and areas of interest in implementing their programmes.

v. It may hamper the spirit of enterprise among individuals in the state

vi. Goods produced may not be of high standard as there is no competition

vii. Economic wastages may occur as a result of allowing unskilled or less efficient workers to handle production.

viii. The masses have to take whatever they are offered as there have not varieties to choose from.

2.12 Welfarism

Welfarism is an economic system in which the government adopts the principle of providing some of the crucial needs of the inhabitants of a state. Any government embarking on welfarism does not just do this in a vacuum; it is usually supported or backed up with the appropriate legislation or enactment (laws) for specific purposes relating to the welfare of every individual dwelling in such a state.

When a state shows great concern, protects and promotes the social and economic well-being of its inhabitants through system of laws against unemployment, old age, ill health, education etc. We say such a state is practising welfarism.

It is not superfluous to say that the welfare of citizens of a state should be the sole responsibility of the government. The welfare of the citizen is supposed to be a must for the government because it is one of the basic responsibilities of the government to its citizens. The money required for such welfarism programmes are provided from the taxes collected from the people, since it is obligatory for every citizen to pay his tax.

Nigeria has implemented some welfare programmes in the past. Such programmes include subsidy on feeding of tertiary institution students in the early 70s to middle 80s, Universal Primary Education (UPE) of the old Western Regional Government, free immunization for pregnant women, subsidy on essential commodities, tuition-free education, provision of bursary to Nigerian higher institution students, free medical services, establishment of National

Directorate of Employment to provide gainful employment for all eligible Nigerians,, subsidy on petroleum products to mention a few.

2.13   Advantages of Welfarism

Among other things, the following are the advantages of welfarism

i.   Welfare programme such as introduction of free immunization for pregnant women helps to reduce child mortality rate and keep the children healthy.

ii.   Welfarism helps to prolong lives of the aged ones as their essential needs are catered for e.g. feeding, shelter and medical.

iii. Welfarism in terms of provision of job opportunities for the jobless and payment of upkeep allowance to the jobless can help to reduce crime in the society.

iv.   Welfare programmes as they relate to education have helped to reduce illiteracy in the country.

v.   Introduction of welfare programmes tends to increase the assistance of the rich/philanthropist to the government in her effort to provide for the masses.

vi.   It guarantees good standard of living for the masses.

vii. It helps to wipe out all sorts of double standards

that characterizes capitalist society.

2.14   Disadvantages of Welfarism

i.   Welfarism is always difficult to plan for especially in a country where the population of the people cannot be ascertained. For example, the Universal Free Primary Education programme failed in the Eastern part of Nigeria because of the under-estimation of the population of the people.

ii.   It may encourage people to be unnecessarily lazy as they are conscious of the fact that whether they work or not they would be catered for. Even those working may decide to retire untimely.

iii.   If not properly handled, it can make the government to go bankrupt. For example, where too many people now depend on the government and the resources are not adequate to meet the demand, the situation may be chaotic.

iv.   It may place unnecessary burden on the people since they are to provide the capital required for implementing the programme. For example, the peasant farmers were heavily taxed to meet the expenses of the old Western Region free education.

v.   Welfarism can discourage the enterprising ability of the people.

vi.   It can lead to emergence of the bourgeoisies who determine who gets what and when and how much in the society. A typical example is the free education programme of the military government which produced emergency contractors who constituted themselves as the ruling elites.

2.15   Revision Questions

i.   Define the term feudalism.

ii.   Discuss how feudalism was practised in the Northern and Western part of Nigeria.

iii.   State the advantages and disadvantages of feudalism.

iv.   Differentiate between the ways feudalism was practised in the Western part of Nigeria from the way it was practised in the Northern part of Nigeria.

v.   What is capitalism?

vi.   How was capitalism introduced to Nigeria?

vii.   State the advantages and disadvantages of capitalism as an economic system.

viii.   Give the concept of socialism

ix.   Mention the essentials of socialist economy

x.   Discuss the essential principles of socialism as

contained in the Communist Manifesto of Karl Marx

xi. Give the reasons why you would prefer socialism to capitalism

xii. State the advantages and disadvantages of socialism.

xiii. Define the term welfarism

xiv. Mention ten policies of the present or past governments that could be regarded as welfare programmes.

xv. Enumerate the advantages and disadvantages of welfarism.

Chapter Three: The Political Economy of Underdevelopment – The Case of Nigeria

3.1   The Concept of Under-development

Under-development can be defined as inability or incapacity on the part of a nation or country to meet the crucial needs of its populace or people due to backwardness in terms of modern industries, scientific discoveries, technological inventions, mal-administration or administrative incompetence, corruption and so on and so forth.

It is a country that lacks the technological "know-how" to develop or tap available natural resources to the benefit of its citizens. In an under-developed country, people rely heavily on imported goods because of the inability to produce most of the needed goods. Even, when there are abundant natural resources in such a country the technology for processing such resources are not available, except through foreign firms that usually enter into asymmetric relationship with the developing countries. It may be possible for an under-developed country to have some industries, but a close look at such industries would show that more often than not, they operate below capacity, part of which includes lack of spare parts, shortage of technical experts and so on and so forth. One way or the other, they lack the required means to operate at full capacity. And it is very likely for many of such industries to fold up after many years of retrogressive performance.

In an under-developed country, certain characteristic features are noticeable. These include:

i. People spending large proportion of their income on food, because their income is so low.

ii. The Gross Domestic Product (GDP) is low.

iii. Subsistence farming is so rampant and this could only feed the individual farmers with little or nothing to sell. This is so because the output of labour in agriculture is low.

iv. Unemployment is rampant and even among the few employed ones; there are cases of under-utilization or redundancy.

v. Technological level is very poor.

vi. Diseases are widespread and infant mortality rate is usually very high. This is due to the fact that people are poorly fed and a lot of people have no access to balanced diet.

vii. Poverty is so pronounced that a lot of people take to begging for their living.

viii. The level of literacy is usually low with education being under-funded

ix. There is incessant strike by workers pressing for good conditions of service.

x. Insufficient industries, constant power failure and inadequate social amenities for the masses.

xi.   Poor medical services with few hospitals.

xii.   Both traditional and modern sectors exist together in a given economy.   That is, the economy is dualistic.

xiii.   The available natural resources are usually under-developed and under-utilized.

3.2   Nigeria and Under-development

It is factual to say that Nigeria is a developing country. However, when it is realized that Nigeria obtained her political independence on 1st of October, 1960, many decades ago, coupled with the available natural resources that the country is endowed with, vis-a-vis the level of development the country has attained, one may rightly say that Nigeria is an under-developed country. Many years after independence, Nigeria is yet to develop any meaningful technology of its own. All she does is to depend on foreign technology, bringing in completely knocked down components and assembling same in Nigeria.

Nigeria is blessed with abundant natural resources but most of the resources have not been exploited due to technological problem. Crude oil exploitation that has received attention of the country is entrusted to foreign firms who signed partnership agreements with the federal government. All other resources like gold, timber, coal.

Bitumen to mention a few that could be found in Nigeria in large quantity are yet to be properly exploited. Sometime, in March 2003, Chief Olusegun Obasanjo who was the then President and Commander-in-Chief of the Armed Forces of the Federal Republic of Nigeria officially launched the commencement of exploitation of bitumen deposit in Agbabu near Ode-Irele, Ondo State. This bitumen deposit has been discovered there many years ago, but the government did not make any meaningful effort to exploit it.

The genesis of under-development in Nigeria could be traced back to the colonial era when Nigeria was initiated into international trade. Nigeria was exporting goods like rubber, coffee, palm oil, cocoa etc. which were in great demand in European countries for their industries. In order to stabilize and make this trade lucrative to the colonialists, marketing boards, which served as a means of appropriation and exploitation, were established. These were used to cheat the peasant farmers as they were being paid lesser amount than the actual value of their produce. The surplus realized from this exploitation was used to develop Europe. One would think that the situation would change after independence, but it is the same story. Nigerians who succeeded the British continued to exploit their fellow Nigerians. Up till today, exploitation, corruption, selfishness, self-centredness are still existing in the nation. That is why there is rarely anything to show for the long period of independence of the nation. All characteristic features of under-development are present in Nigeria.

It is highly regrettable that Nigeria which is one of the leading world producers of crude oil was at a time ranked by the United Nations Development Programme (UNDP), in its Human Development Index as the 15th poorest country in the world.

Some past rulers of the country (both military and civilian) impoverished the nation through their corrupt practices. As observed by Asoga Allen (2000), there is rarely any regime in Nigeria where people did not steal the nation's money. If the stolen money had been invested in Nigeria, it would have helped the economy of the nation to grow as Nigerians would have been employed, but these stolen funds were banked abroad. All these nefarious and unpatriotic actions of some past leaders helped to strengthen the economy of those countries where such money were banked. They loan it to their people for various development projects while the people in the country where the money had been stolen are groaning in poverty and penury. The technology being used in most industries in Nigeria is imported from foreign countries. In terms of technological development, Nigeria is nowhere to be found in the world. Even common storage technology has not been developed in Nigeria. That is why we have seasons of surplus and scarcity of certain agricultural produce, while the technological developed countries like United States of America, United Kingdom, Japan etc, the surplus produce are preserved throughout the year thereby making life easy for the populace as they enjoy stable price.

The government has made various pronouncements in the past concerning technological growth of the nation and several plans and proposals have been made but none of these has been given a down to earth attention needed. The Universities of Science and Technology established in various parts of Nigeria have not been able to develop as expected because they are not properly funded. And it is a clear fact that no nation can develop scientifically and technologically if the tertiary institutions and research institutes are neglected and poorly funded.

3.3   Basic Requirements for Economic Development

For the economy of an under-developed country to develop, certain social, economic, psychological and cultural requirements must be put in place. Such requirements include:

i.   **Indigenous base**: This simply means that the step towards making life better for the people or improving the standard of living of the people must come from the indigenes themselves, rather than from foreigners. Though foreigners may participate in this process, but should not be the major player. This is because no nation can love another nation more than it loves itself. And man is the major architect of his fortune or misfortune.

ii.   **Removal of market imperfection**: The economy of an under-developed nation would do better if government could reduce her intervention in the market to the barest minimum. In this wise, private individuals should be encouraged to produce or participate in producing goods and services. The idea of subsidizing everything in a developing economy is harmful to economic growth. That is why the privatization and commercialization programme of the government is mostly welcomed, but it has to be properly handled so that the few rich in the society would not buy all the nation's parastatals and thereafter descend on the masses with high prices of goods and services and make life unbearable for them. Government should make it possible for ordinary workers to buy shares from these parastatals so that it would not be dominated by the few rich alone. Except this is done, it may amount to selling the nation to few unscrupulous individuals whose sources of income are questionable and are capable of doing more harm to the economy than good.

iii.   **Structural changes**: For an under-developed economy to grow and develop, there is need for structural change of the economy. That is, the economy must change from being agro-based to modern industrial-based with a radical transformation of existing institutions, social attitudes and motivation. For such changes to be meaningful, it must be capable of increasing employment opportunities, Gross Domestic Products (GDP) and Per Capita Income. All these are lacking in the various adjustment programmes of the past governments in Nigeria. Most of the changes embarked upon in the past have only helped to worsen the situation and throw the people into more economic hardships.

iv.   **Capital formation**: For an under-developed economy to pick up, there is need for capital formation. Capital formation is an important factor or key to economic growth. These could be done in three inter-dependent ways:

a.   By increasing the volume of savings which is based on willingness to save and the ability to save.

b.   By putting credit and financial institutions in place

c.   By ensuring returns on the savings in terms of the rate of interest

3.4   Revision Questions

i.   Define the term under-development

ii.   Enumerate the characteristic features of under-development

iii.   Adduce reasons for the under-development of Nigeria

iv.   Discuss the basic requirements for economic development.

Chapter Four: The Political Economy of Poverty – Nigeria as a Case Study

4.1   The Concept of Poverty

Poverty may be defined as a condition of not being able to meet one's demand for the basic necessities of life. It has been stressed by the economists that human wants are numerous and insatiable. That is, no sooner you satisfy your want for one thing than another want takes its place. This assertion not-with-standing, there are basic necessities of life which are crucial to man. These include food, clothing and shelter. Except man is able to meet these needs, he may find it difficult to survive. Man works to be able to satisfy his needs, even though it is difficult to satisfy all his needs at the same time, he picks the most important one first, and as he satisfies this, he moves to the next important one. In essence, man would continue to have needs as long as he lives. No matter the economic status of man in the society, he would still be in need of one thing or the other.

Poverty in the real sense of it is when one is not able to make ends meet. He finds it difficult to have three square meals in a day, cannot cloth himself, or provide shelter for his family. Poverty is fast becoming a serious disease in Africa, Asia and Latin America where a lot of people live in abject poverty. As far as Nigeria is concerned, poverty is a national disaster, majority of the populace find it difficult to have three square meals in a day. The effects of poverty are felt by both young and old, workers and students. The situation in Nigeria is an indication that one could be inside water and be thirsty or possess all the resources and still be poor. Nigeria is naturally blessed with abundant natural resources. It is no more news that Nigeria is one of the leading oil producing countries of the world. In fact, Nigeria was ranked the 6th largest oil producer in the world, but income from crude oil has not made any significant impact on the living standard of Nigerians. Nigerian workers are one of the poorest paid workers in the world. Though, the situation changed a bit when Chief Olusegun Obasanjo became civilian president in 1999, he approved good salary for workers, but the joy of this was short lived with incessant increase of fuel price. It sounds highly ridiculous to know that a university graduate earned less than N3000 in 1998.

Millions of Nigerian school leavers roam the street without job. The higher institutions in Nigeria turn out graduates every year without any plan on how the graduates would be employed. During the military regime the commonest thing was embargo on employment. It is commonsensical to match increase in enrolment of schools/colleges/universities with increase in job opportunities. In fact, that is what is done in developed countries. A situation where people are admitted into higher institutions yearly without any budget for job creation is very dangerous for the nation. The effects of this have started to be felt in Nigeria on the area of crime. It is now rampant for graduates to be caught in robbery. The step being taken by the government is to recruit more policemen to tackle crimes rather than treating the causes of crimes in Nigeria. Lives of police officers are being exposed to danger. Many were killed on a daily basis because the robbers carried superior weapons.

4.2 Reasons for Poverty in Nigeria and Africa

Strivastina (1975) described poverty as a class of under-privileged. He stressed further that inequality in terms of access has been one of the major causes of poverty. Bhagwat (1976), commenting on poverty says that, "While a few countries are greatly wealthy, nearly two-thirds of the world population live on substandard income". He stated further that illiteracy, bad housing, lack of medical care and malnutrition are prevalent throughout most of Asia, Africa, the Middle East and Latin America. As earlier said, Nigeria was ranked the 15th poorest nation of the world according to the UNDP Human Development Index some years ago.

Poverty in Nigeria or African could be attributed to the following:

i.   **Bad leadership**: Since independence, it seems Nigeria has not been fortunate to have a good leader who is determined to serve his people meritoriously and have his name written in gold. Experiences have shown that corruption which Nigeria was initially rated first in the whole world and later second after Bangladesh, in 1999 and 2000 has its roots in the high places. Most Nigerian past and present leaders seem to place self interest above national interest. They love money more than their names. This reflects in the way they engage themselves in corrupt practices in order to get rich quickly. While many of them accumulate what they and their third or fourth generations cannot exhaust, those that they rule are wallowing in poverty. The worst part is that they have formed themselves into the ruling class by virtue of their ill-gotten wealth.

ii. **Mal-administration or administrative incompetence**: The Nigerian economy has been badly managed over the years by incompetent leaders. Politics in Nigeria is a dirty game. People play money politics. Once you have the money and you are able to bribe your way through, even though you have nothing upstairs to render, people would vote for you. In retrospect, those who are good administrators and highly educated have not been allowed to get to the top. It is unimaginable that a person who did not possess a minimum of first degree could be voted as president of a large country like Nigeria. We have seen in the past where a leader who had no knowledge of administration and could rarely understand any accounting procedure was voted as president. When any budget or requisition was placed before him, he would just append his signature. No sooner he was sworn in than the nation's account entered red. Some ministers in his administration started to purchase jet planes, in addition to their chains of expensive cars. Some of the Generals that ruled the nation through "coup d'état" were quota system Generals. Many of whom are not supposed to be above the rank of a Colonel. But because promotion in the Army was based on quota system, they were promoted whether they merited such promotion or not just to fill the quota of their geographical zone. How do you expect such Generals who could only manage to read and write to be in charge of the economy of a nation like Nigeria? All they succeeded in doing was to steal billions of naira belonging to the nation and banked same abroad. A lot of Nigeria stolen money wasted in foreign banks till today. All the efforts of the government to recover the money have not been successful. Some of the government of foreign nations where this money is kept are reluctant to support the idea of Nigeria recovering the money. This is because of the benefit derivable or being derived from such money (Asoga-Allen, 1996)

iii.   **Technological Backwardness**: For a nation to

grow and develop, the place of technological advancement cannot be over-emphasized. Technology in this sense has to do with application of scientific ideas and discoveries to solve human problems and to provide human needs.

When God created heaven and earth and all that are in it, everything appeared in a natural state. It is obvious that the early man did not enjoy most of those things we are enjoying today because of the level of technology then. Before he discovered how to make fire, the early man eats his food raw and struggle with lower animals for food. During that time, there was no textile, no modern planes to mention a few. It is through scientific discoveries that all these things are now put in place.

Technological development brings about industrialization. In an industrialized nation, employment opportunities are available for the populace as people produce not only for consumption but also export to earn foreign exchange

Developed countries like United States of American (USA), United Kingdom (UK), Japan, Germany etc to mention a few are able to attain their level of development through scientific discoveries and technological development. African countries are yet to come out with any meaningful technology. Most of the industries in Africa apply technologies transferred from developed countries. Due to this problem of technological backwardness, there were little opportunities for Nigerians in terms of employment prospects. If there is mechanised farming, for instance, a lot of people could be engaged in farming, but this is not in place because Nigeria has not been able to manufacture farming tools/equipment needed for such project. That is the reason for competition among school leavers/graduates for white collar job. And there is limited number of people that could be employed in government services. This problem also affect other African countries.

iv. **Imperialism**: This has to do with imperialist influences on the economy of a nation. The imperialist influence on Nigerian economy in the colonial days helped to impoverish the nation. The imperialists came to Nigeria and indeed other African countries for two things namely, raw materials and market for finished goods. This idea was supported by Aschcraft (1973), when he comments that : "the metropolitan countries in their struggle for growth sought to find a source of raw materials and a ready market for manufactured goods".

The imperialists were after their personal gains not what the African countries could gain. Onimode (1993) noted that domination, inequality and exploitation characterized imperialism. According to him, imperialists exploitation involved appropriation of the economic surplus of one country by another through enslavement, forced labour, low wages, acquisition of mineral rights, land alienation and so on and so forth, all of which generated high profits for the imperialists.

Some of the means employed by imperialists to perpetuate their exploitation in the economy of most developing countries include violence, trade, foreign investment, aid/grant as well as international organizations like IMF, World Bank to mention a few.

v.   **Corruption**: This is a major canker worm that has eaten deep into bones and marrow of most Nigerians. There is corruption both in high and low places (Oyeneye, 1997). Initially, corruption was only heard of at the top, but today it is a national phenomenon. There is no gain-saying, the fact that the economic problem most Nigerians are facing today is a consequence of corrupt activities of some past leaders that ruled the nation. As earlier mentioned, billions of Nigerian stolen money is stashed in foreign banks. One is highly optimistic that if all stolen Nigerian money is recovered, it is enough to make life better for Nigerians and ensure an improved standard of living in Nigeria.

Corruption is not confined to Nigeria alone, some other African countries are groaning under the bondage of poverty due to the corrupt practices of their past and present leaders. Ghana is a typical example. Flight Lt. Jerry Rawlings, former President of Ghana ordered the execution of some past Ghanaian leaders who corruptly enriched themselves. There was a time when Ghanaians trooped to many other African countries in search of jobs as a result of poor economy of their country then.

vi.   **Military intervention in politics**: Anytime the military seize power from a democratically elected government, the society is thrown into confusion. Things became abnormal. The usual first step by them is to suspend the constitution and start to dish out decrees. The military are not trained to rule; rather they have their traditional duty as defending the nation against external attack. Nigeria, like most African countries, has passed through long period of military rule. The military has dominated the rulership of Nigeria since independence. This has made a lot of foreign investments to elude the nation. It is a basic fact that no nation would like to invest in an unstable environment, more so when the duration of such illegal government could not be determined. In the past, it was "soldier goes soldier comes". The worst part is that when one military overthrows another military government, they rarely follow the policy of the previous government. Each new government comes up with new policies that would help it achieve its selfish ambition.

vii.   **Elite-oriented programmes**: Most of the policies and programmes being embarked upon by African governments are those ones that are designed to benefit the rich and not the poor. Take for instance, the building programmes of some state governments and even the Federal Government of Nigeria. The impression being created is that the houses are being built for low income earners but after completing the building, they sell for as much as five or six million naira. Should we say that a house that is sold for five or six million naira is for low income earners? Or how many Nigerian workers can boast of five hundred thousand naira of their own? You would discover that such houses are bought by the same class of people (the rich).

Another example is the National Agricultural Development Programme (NADP) of the Federal Government, where some tractors are procured to be hired out to peasant farmers, and they ask them to pay outrageous amount each day they use it. Where can the peasant farmers get such an amount? One would discover that only the rich farmers could afford such sum.

viii.   **Laziness**: This is another major cause of poverty. Some people are naturally lazy, they do not like to work. They believe that government has to provide all their needs. This attitude is peculiar to some people in the oil producing area of the country. The belief is that the resources are from their area, people do not need to work again. It is obvious that if someone is not working and you continue to give him money, the money may not last in his hand because he would not know the labour involved before the money is got.

With the situation of the country, there are still a lot of legitimate activities that one could engage in to earn one's living. When some Ghanaians came to Nigeria in the early 80s, they engaged in various activities like shoe shining, sowing, tailoring, truck pushing, driving and so on and so forth and they made a lot of money from it. It is a wrong idea to say that except one is able to secure an office job, he/she would not work. If one cannot secure what he wants, he has to take what he gets. One should not at anytime allow himself to be idle, because an idle hand is the devil's workshop. And a man that does not work is not qualified to eat. It is great wisdom for one to do something that fetches him money every day no matter the situation of the job. Money obtained from packing faeces does not smell.

ix.   **Neo-colonialism**: It is true that all African countries are independent and they enjoy their sovereignty to some extent. However, they are still being controlled by their former colonial masters. In case of Nigeria, the British handed over power to those whom they felt would be able to protect their economic interest and who would always dance to their tunes.

It is a basic fact that most African countries today, depend on their former colonial masters who dictate to them their economic policies and programmes. In a situation like that, you could imagine the type of programme they would want the people to embark on. A Yoruba adage says "if you give a hoe to even a mad man, he would heap the sand to his own side".

x.   **Agro-based economy**: At least about seventy five percent (75%) of Nigerian population engage in agriculture. The type of agriculture being practised in Nigeria is the type that could be described as "hand-to-mouth" agriculture (subsistence farming). The farming is limited to what the farmers and his immediate family could do alone in terms of labour since mechanized farming is not yet in existence in most parts of Nigeria.

This type of farming only produces food for the farmer and his family. They rarely get much to take to the market. Even where a farmer tries to expand his farmland – perhaps he obtains loan from the government, at harvest, he has to sell his produce cheaply to prevent them from spoiling due to lack of storage facilities. In essence, farming in Nigeria has not been fetching farmers enough money as expected and this discourages people from going into farming. People see farming as an occupation that requires more and pay less.

In some African countries where mechanised farming is being practised e.g. Kenya, South Africa, most of the mechanised farmers are white men. The black have no means to embark on such projects.

4.3   Poverty eradication in Nigeria and Africa

The following steps would help to eradicate poverty in Nigeria or Africa:

i.   Democracy should be enthroned throughout the African continent as the only approved system of government. Military should not be allowed in governance and in fact, military government should not be recognised anywhere in Africa.

ii.   Africans should screen properly those they would elect to rule them. People with dubious character, should not be allowed to hold any leadership position in the society.

iii.   Nigerians should not rest until they succeed in recovering all the stolen money stashed in foreign banks by the past Nigerian leaders, because there is no doubt that , if this money is recovered, Nigerians would overcome the economic problems facing them easily. There would be economic transformation in the country.

iv.   Whoever, would be elected as president of the Federal Republic of Nigeria must be somebody who have succeeded in managing an organization whether (private or public), not a novice who is not known anywhere with any tangible success but presented by an ethnic group or geographical zone because of zoning of political offices. This is because experience have shown that zoning system have produced candidates with low mentality and mediocre.

v.   The Independent Corrupt Practices Commission (ICPC) should be allowed to stay and be given free hands to work. It is a basic fact that for corruption to be wiped out of Nigeria, a lot of heads will roll, but if that is what it takes to purge the nation of this anti-progress disease, there should be no going back. It has to be pursued to a logical conclusion

vi.   Efforts should be directed towards scientific and

technological development. Nigerian scientists should wake up from their slumber and the government should be ready to always support and finance scientific discoveries. We have to start somewhere; it is a serious abnormality if a child of 52 years is still crawling.

vii.   A lot of jobs would be created in the agricultural sector if government could import the necessary equipment and embark on mechanized farming. If food is out of poverty, poverty has already been reduced to the barest minimum. Mechanized farming would not only make the nation self-sufficient in food production but also would make the nation one of the food exporting nations of the world. Commodities like cocoa, cotton, coffee, palm oil etc that the country was known for in the past should not be forgotten. They should be cultivated in large scale. This would widen the avenue for generating more income through foreign exchange earnings for the country.

viii.   Nigerian leaders should free themselves from foreign domination and should bear in mind that no nation would come and develop African nation or could love African nations more than the Africans; no foreigner would come and develop Africa for the Africans. The initiative to develop Africa must come from the Africans; Therefore, African leaders should remain focused and plan the growth of Africa by shunning all forms of foreign interferences and dependency on foreign aid/assistance. Though, assistance may be received, there is nothing bad in it; but to always rely on other nations for assistance is a shameful habit.

ix.   According to Asoga-Allen (2000), reasonable amount of money should henceforth be budgeted for job generation and creation annually to cater for unemployed graduates. Money should be made available for people to go into various fields, not necessarily office jobs alone.

x.   Any corrupt leader should be treated like armed robber, robbery is robbery, whether it is done by arms or with pen, they both have the same consequences.

xi.   The interest of the poor masses should be paramount and constantly be in the minds of African leaders, and to this end, only programmes that would benefit the masses should be embarked upon, not programmes that would make the rich to be richer and the poor to be poorer (capitalist programmes or elite-oriented programmes).

xii. Africans/Nigerians should imbibe the culture of hard work and commitment to one's duty. Being hardworking is the remedy to poverty, a lazy man has no place in the society, in fact, he is an unproductive and an economic liability to his nation.

4.4   Revision Questions

i.   Define the term poverty

ii. Give reasons for high level poverty in Nigeria or Africa

iii. Suggest means by which the problem of poverty could be surmounted

Chapter Five: Political Economy of Cultural Development

5.1 The Concept of Culture

Culture may be conceptualised as the totality of the way of life of a people. According to Litton (1995), the culture of a society is the way of life of its members, the collection of ideas and habit which they learn, share and transmit from generation to generation. Kluckhoh (1951) has an elegant definition of culture. He says it is a design for living held by members of a particular society. Since man has an instinct to direct his actions like animals, his behaviour therefore must be based on guidelines, which are learnt. In order to enhance the effective operation of the society, the guideline must be shared and adhered to by its members (Asoga-Allen, 2000).

Culture has two basic attributes: Firstly, it is learned; and secondly, it is shared. It is pertinent to say that without a shared culture, it would be difficult, if not impossible for the society to communicate and cooperate.

To confirm that culture is learned, Akbar who was an India Emperor between 1542 -1602 decreed that a group of children be brought up without receiving any language instruction. This was to test the belief that such children would certainly or eventually speak Hebrew, the language of God. At the end, the children developed no spoken language communication. This experiment of Akbar confirmed that fact that language as part of culture is learned. To a greater extent, culture determines how members of a society think and feel. It also directs their actions and defines their outlook of life. Man does not just behave anyhow; it is the culture that defines accepted ways of behaviour for members of a particular society. For a behaviour to be deemed acceptable, it must be in consonance with the culture of a particular society.

5.2   Nigerian Cultural Objectives

The Cultural Policy for Nigeria (CPN, 1988) showed clearly the objectives of Nigerian cultural development. Among other things, it includes:

a.   Mobilizing and motivating the people by disseminating and propagating ideas which promote national pride, solidarity and consciousness;

b.   Evolving from our plurality, a national culture which will reflect in African and world affairs;

c.   Promoting an educational system that motivates, stimulates creativity and draws largely on our tradition and values;

d.   Promoting creativity in the fields of arts, science and technology, and ensuring the continuity of traditional skills and sports and their progressing updating to serve modern development needs as our contribution to world growth of culture and ideas; and

e.   Enhancing national self-reliance and self-sufficiency and national industrialization.

5.3   Ways of Achieving Nigerian Cultural Objectives

Nigerian cultural policy could be implemented and the objectives could be achieved through the following steps:

i.   **Informal education**: This is the type of education given to a child outside the classroom. Parents, brothers, sisters, elderly ones in the society give informal education to the children. In those days or in a traditional African society, the child belongs to the society, not to the biological parents alone as it is the situation in the present days. If everyone in the society makes it a duty to educate the young ones, the way they should behave or pattern of behaviour in the society, the young ones would imbibe the culture of the society.

ii.   **Formal education**: This is the type of education that is given to the child within the four walls of a school. It is planned and systematic and there are specially trained teachers who impart the knowledge. Also, there is a special syllabus to follow. If Nigerian culture is included in the school curriculum and taught in schools, there is no doubt that our cultural policy and objectives would be achieved.

iii. **Documentation of our culture**: This is a way of documenting our culture into video cassettes, video CD for the incoming generations. It is very important to give accurate information. The recording should be devoid of embellishments. If this is done, the incoming generation would see things physically rather than being told, and would be able to follow the same.

iv. **Establishment of monumental centres/museums**: This would serve as a place where our cultural materials are kept. It would help to protect the artefacts of historical significance and monumental structures.

v. **Annual celebration of cultural festivals**: Celebrating culture at the national, state and local levels annually would help in the achievement of the nation's cultural objectives. During such celebrations each state should be represented and should be allowed to display their cultural heritage.

vi. **Budgetary allocation to culture**: Enough money should be budgeted to culture annually at the three tiers of government. Cultural activities should be promoted and encouraged, if this is done, it would develop people's interest in their culture.

vii.   The media houses should give cultural programmes great publicity. In fact, their programmes should reflect not less than 50% of the nation's culture. In essence, emphasis should be on indigenous culture rather than foreign culture as it is the case today.

viii.   **Encouraging tourism**: This would help people to visit other places and imbibe their culture.

ix.   **Functional enlightenment campaigns**: There should be functional enlightenment campaigns going on in the nation on culture. This would remind the general public of the need to train their young ones about their culture and to handle the issue of culture seriously.

5.4   Revision Questions

a.   Define the term culture

b.   State the objectives of culture in Nigeria

c.   Suggest ways by which Nigerian cultural objectives could be achieved

d.   Can Nigerians be regarded as people who have culture today? Give reasons for your answer.

Chapter Six: Political Economy of Population, Women and Child Welfare

6.1 The Concept of Population

Population refers to the number of people living in a place. It may be a village, town, state or country depending on the area to be covered. Population includes both the young and old, male and female living in a particular place.

The world population means the number of people living in the world. The rate of population explosion in Africa is higher than that of the western world. In the western world, you find a couple having two children, three or maximum of four, but in Africa, it is a common phenomenon for a man to marry eight wives with about thirty or forty children.

This population explosion has economic consequences. Increase in Nigerian population has increased government financial commitments in the areas of education, transportation, health and employment. An increase in population that is not accompanied by increase in economic growth and development is dangerous to a nation. The nation's economic planning must focus on population increase and how to cater for them.

It seems there is no meaningful economic planning in Nigeria, and if there is one that means it has not been followed. For instance, cities like Lagos, Ibadan, Benin etc. have population explosion and social amenities are not enough to cope with the increasing population. Infrastructural facilities are not enough. Most of the areas cannot enjoy medical facilities of the government because of the distance and the number of people patronising the existing ones. There is no pipe borne water in most areas and where this is found, the number of people using it is more than the supply.

The situation in the rural area is worse. No social amenities like pipe-borne water, electricity, telecommunication facilities etc. in most of the rural areas. Industries are not in most of the rural areas where the school leavers can work. No access road, no job opportunities, no place of attraction that is why there is mass rural-urban migration.

6.2   Women and Child Welfare

Women play important roles in the life of a nation. Biologically, women gave birth to children that later become adults. With the level of scientific discoveries in the world, no one has been able to produce a complete human being without passing through a woman. It is a common belief that a healthy woman would produce a healthy child. Women need to be taken adequate care of, if we want to produce children who are mentally sound and are capable of contributing to national development.

In addition to child bearing, the women play significant and indispensable roles to both man and child. When the man has gone to work, the woman prepares the food for the family, takes good care of the children and washes the dresses of the family. She is a counsellor to the man and the child. "A virtuous woman is a crown to the husband", says the Holy Bible. In some parts of the world, women are not allowed to participate in any economic activity; they are made full-time house wives due to religious reasons. In other countries women are being marginalized. They do not have equal rights with men. African countries are typical example where education of women suffered a lot of setback in the olden days. Women were rarely sent to school. The general belief then was that women would end up in another man's house. However, the trend has changed in modern time, women are now being sent to school and after graduation they are employed to work in the same office with men.

In Nigeria, certain key positions were reserved for men in the past. Women were not allowed to get into such positions. But in recent time, the situation has changed. However, it took a lot of struggle among Nigerian women before they could attain the present level. In Nigeria today, women are found in top positions and they compete with their men counterparts as achievers. The one time

Comptroller-General of immigration was a woman. Also the former Director General of National Agency for Food, Drug, Administration and Control (NAFDAC) was a woman. In the politics women are not lagging behind. In 1999 elections in Nigeria, women emerged as Deputy Governors, some were appointed as Commissioners and others Ministers/Directors. It is interesting to note that in 2003 general election women contested with men for various positions e.g. Presidency, Governorship, and House of Representative/Senate.

A lot still need be done to bring Nigerian women to the same level with their male counterparts. For example, a lot of women are still languishing in poverty due to inability to secure fund. Women are knowledgeable and they have flair for business but are incapacitated by lack of money.

Many women have been turned to child bearing machines by their husbands and they are treated like unimportant tools that are only good for the kitchen and to satisfy their sexual and childbearing desires. This is common among the illiterates. A lot of programmes have been put in place by the present and past Nigerian governments to better the lots of women. Such programmes included the Better Life for Rural Women, Women Empowerment and others. However, much success has not been achieved by these various programmes due to selfishness, insincerity and corruption that have characterized the nation. Most of the materials meant for rural women end up in the hands of urban women.

In the area of healthcare, Nigerian women have not received adequate care like their counterparts in the other parts of the world. The rate at which women died during childbirth is still very high. Something needs to be done in this direction to save Nigerian women from unnecessary labour and untimely death during childbirth.

Children are the leaders of tomorrow and the type of leaders a country would have in future depends on the children of today. A child that is healthy and well fed would develop into a competent and reasonable adult. Unfortunately, Nigerian children are victims of the economic hardship facing their parents. Some are so poorly fed that their growth is retarded. Some die of disease like Kwashiorkor as a result of lack of balanced diet.

Most Nigerian children are still being subjected to forced labour and enslavement because of the poverty facing their parents. It is regrettable that a bill forwarded to the National Assembly by Chief Olusegun Obasanjo in 2002 on the rights of Nigerian child was politicised and thrown out by those that were elected to represent us. It is a fact that Nigeria is a signatory to the world Convention on the rights of children but she has not taken any desirable step to guarantee the rights of Nigerian children. A lot of Nigerian children still die during birth. The child's welfare in terms of medical health in Nigeria is nothing to write home about. One is optimistic that the situation would get better especially in these days of enthronement of democracy in Nigeria. Also the rejected bill on the rights of Nigerian child was represented to the National Assembly and was eventually passed into law.

6.3   Political Economy of Resource Development and Allocation

It is a basic fact that Nigeria is endowed with abundant natural resources. Some of these resources are yet to be developed due to lack of the needed technology. Even, those that could be said to have been developed are done through foreign partners and technological transfer. Nigeria has not been able to single headedly tap the available resources and this has greatly affected the income of the country as we have to share the profit with the technical partners.

The crude oil which is an economic backbone of Nigeria could not be said to have been exploited to the satisfaction and full comfort of Nigerians. Fifty two (52) years after independence, Nigeria is having four refineries; these refineries are still being maintained by foreign partners. That is why they could not operate at full capacity. The effect of this is that, Nigeria exports crude oil to foreign countries and import refined petrol from those countries. From time to time Nigerians face scarcity of petrol, diesel, oil and kerosene and during such periods, economic activities are paralysed as motorists spent most of their time in the fuel station.

Other resources that would have fetched the nation a lot of foreign exchange are neglected. For example, bitumen was discovered in Nigeria more than one hundred years ago, it was only in the 90s that Chief Olusegun Obasanjo officially launched a programme for its exploitation. Previous government in Nigeria had not seen any need to exploit it.

Another resource is agriculture. Before the discovery of crude oil in Nigeria, Nigeria was famous for cocoa, as well as palm oil, timber, groundnut and coffee production. All these commodities were fetching the country a lot of foreign exchange. But with the advent of crude oil, all these agricultural produce were neglected. Nigeria is blessed with fertile land. It is a basic fact that Nigeria is capable of surviving as a nation with extensive agriculture or mechanised farming without crude oil. In fact, a lot of Nigerians would have earned their living through this means. The crude oil business that has occupied the full attention of the nation has not generated enough employment for Nigerians.

Income from this crude oil that could have been used to generate employment was not properly accounted for in the past due to some unscrupulous, selfish and dishonest leaders that ruled the nation.

In Nigeria, all resources belong to the Federal Government no matter the area where they are found. The constitution of Nigeria confers the power to exploit natural resources on the Federal Government. Though, the area where such resources are found is recognised, it cannot claim ownership of such resources. Also no state or local government is empowered to tap or control the resources found in her territory. To compensate such areas where resources are tapped, there is a constitutional provision that 13% of federally generated income on such resources be given to the areas where such resources are tapped. This is called derivation fund. All the states where crude oil is found in Nigeria benefit from this, in addition to general share from the federation account.

It is the Federal Government that allocates fund to all other tiers of government. It does this through committee known as Revenue Mobilization Allocation and Fiscal Commission. This commission is responsible for recommending formula for allocation as well as allocation of fund to the three tiers of government. As at present, the Federal Government takes the lion's share of the income from federation accounts. Next to the federal government is the state government, and the least is the local government.

The state especially, the southern states are still struggling with the Federal Government to hands off the control of resources find in their jurisdiction to them. This has landed both of them in court at a time. The law relating to resource control was interpreted in favour of the Federal Government. In fact, except the constitution is amended, it may not be easy for the state to enjoy such control as it is against the federal constitution of Nigeria.

6.4   Revision Questions

i.   What is population?

ii.   Discuss the effect of population explosion on the economy of Nigeria

iii.   Of what importance is woman in the family?

iv.   State the problems facing Nigerian women and suggest means by which the problems could be tackled

v.   State the problems facing the Nigerian children and suggest means by which these problems could be solved

vi.   Discuss the situation of resource development and allocation in Nigeria

vii.   Discuss how resources could be fully developed and utilized in Nigeria

viii.   Who should control resources, state or federal?

Chapter Seven: Science and Technology in Society

7.1 The Concepts of Science, Technology and Society

To a layman, science is everything that enhances and sustains comfort and happiness. Most scientists see science as intellectual activity which enables man to understand nature. Science has to do with identification of problem, finding out the causes and how the problem could be solved.

Man is faced with a lot of natural and artificial problems in his environment, thus, there is need to surmount the problems and make the environment conducive and habitable for man. That is where science comes in. Every society struggles and evolves appropriate technology for solving its problems. This is done through intensification of efforts on scientific research and discoveries.

Science is an intellectual exercise geared towards identification of natural and artificial problems of man by diagnosing and synthesising the problems in order to discover the causes as well as the appropriate means of solving them. Man works on the environment and converts the environment to the form that is comfortable for him.

Olutimehin (1995), quoting Conant, an American scientist, defines science as interconnected series of concepts and conceptual schemes that have developed as a result of experimentation and observation and are fruitful for further experimentation and observations. Scientific knowledge is gained through scientific research, for example, observation, experimentation and testing. It is relevant to say that scientific knowledge or fact is empirical. They are provable and verifiable.

In science, there is no absolute fact; rather, any fact discovered is subject to modification or rejection when new facts emerge. Science could be said to embrace the following:

i. **Attitude**: That is, certain beliefs, values, opinion e.g. postponing decision making until enough data are collected on the problem at stake.

ii. **Processes/Methods**: That is, there are certain ways of conducting scientific investigations e.g. identification of problem, formulation of hypothesis, designing and carrying out experiment, data evaluation etc.

iii. **Products**: That is, facts, principles, laws,

theories for example a scientific principle is that which says when metals are heated, they expand (Olutimehin, 1995). Only facts that are verifiable could be said to be science. There is interconnectivity of events in science, that is, it is a belief that no event happens in isolation without being caused by another event.

Technology

Technology may be defined as the application of scientific knowledge gained from scientific research to solve human problem. Scientific facts are acquired through scientific research. When the facts or knowledge is applied to solve human problem or produce human needs, it becomes a technology. For example, headache is a sickness that troubles man. Through scientific research, scientific facts emerged on how to produce tablets that can cure headache. When these facts are directed towards producing tablets like paracetamol, cafenol etc. It becomes a technology. Technology is the means or method used to produce something.

Another example of technology is the invention of motor car. Before motor car was invented, man was faced with the problem of trekking a long distance or travelling from one place to another. Through scientific research facts emerged on how to design a locomotive engine. When these facts were applied to the invention of cars, motorcycle etc., then technology emerged. When scientific research is applied to a situation, it changes the situation to the form desired by man. All the man-made things enjoyed by man in the environment e.g. car, buildings, tools, textiles etc required technology for making them and the technology was arrived at as a result of scientific researches.

Society

Ezewu (1981) observes that individual in groups does not exist in isolation, but exists with other members of the group and their interaction follow some laid-down patterns of behaviour that are acceptable to the group. All these interacting individuals and groups, with their activities exist in a larger set up called society. According to Asoga-Allen (2000), the society embraces human beings, their activities and relationship to one another and to the natural and social environment. It is therefore possible to talk or refer to tribal society e.g. Hausa society, Idoma society, Yoruba society etc. Each of these societies has specific references to their physical environment.

A society according to Ijaduola (1996), is a group of

people who share a common culture, tradition, language and physical environment. The Nigerian society is a collection of these groups of people.

7.2   Differences between Science and Technology

It is difficult, if not impossible, to divorce science from technology. Science has to do with identification of problem, reasoning and thinking out how the problem could be solved by going through scientific processes e.g. formulation of hypothesis, collection of data, experimentation etc.   until facts are discovered. Technology has to do with the application of scientific facts or knowledge to solve an identified problem. It is worthy of note that science comes first before technology. In fact, without scientific research there cannot be technology. It is the scientific research that gives birth to technology.   Thus, science and technology go *pari-pasu*. It is rational to say that technology is the product of scientific research. Technology cannot develop without science. For instance, having a biological weapon (BW) is a sign of technological advancement in military of any nation. This has taken its root from an aspect of science i.e microbiology. Also having a chemical weapon (CW) programme is another indication of technological advancement in warfare of any nation at present. It is the end product of chemistry, which is an area of science.

7.3   Development of Science and Technology in Nigeria

The Nigerian government has been trying to promote science and technology. This has been done by setting up organisations that formulate and monitor the implementation of policies on science. The first was in 1970 when the Nigerian Council for Science and Technology (NCST) was established. Also in 1970 the National Research Council for Agriculture and Medicine (NRCAM) was established. In 1977, the NCST became the National Science and Technology Development Agency (NSTDA). Also in 1979, it became the Ministry of Science and Technology. Also established were the Federal Institute of Industrial Research and Federal Institute of Medical Research. The Federal Ministry of Science and Technology came out with the National Policy on Science and Technology as follows:

☐   To increase public awareness in science and technology and their vital role in national development and well-being;

☐   Directing science and technology effort along with unidentified national goals;

☐   Promoting the translation of science and technology results into actual goods and services;

☐ Creating increasing and maintaining an indigenous science and technology base through research and development;

☐ Motivating creative output in science and technology;

☐ Increasing and strengthening theoretical and practical science base in the society;

☐ Increasing and strengthening science and technology base of the nation (Federal Ministry of Information, 1986).

As laudable as the above policy is, it is a pity that Nigeria is yet to have her name written in the record of scientific and technologically advanced nations, because Nigeria is yet to develop technologically. That is why the nation depends largely on the technologies developed in the advanced countries of the world. The level of scientific and technological growth of a nation determines its strength. This explains why some countries are classified as advanced and others developing countries. There is no way by which a country which is yet to develop her science and technology can claim to be strong.

Technology is needed in all spheres of human life and in human environment to make the environment habitable and life worth living for man. Man has applied technology to various parts of his environment.

Some of the areas where man has applied technology include building of houses, construction of roads and bridges, production of medicine, invention of cars, aeroplanes/helicopters, farming to mention a few.

7.4   Problems Facing Nigeria's Scientific and Technological Development

Nigeria has not been able to achieve its objectives of scientific and technological development due to the following problems:

i.   **Lack of adequate finance**: This is one of the major problems facing Nigeria that is yearning for scientific and technological development. Scientific research is capital intensive. It needs capital. Enough priority has not been given to science and technological advancement when preparing budget for each fiscal year. As a result of poor funding, Nigeria scientists have not done much as they are financially handicapped.

ii.   **Lack of encouragement by government to scientists and talented artisans**:   This is another problem hampering scientific growth and development in Nigeria. The scientists and local artisans who succeeded in inventing one thing or the other are not encouraged by the government. For example, there was a time when science students of Kwara State Polytechnic, Ilorin designed a proto-type radio station that was transmitting live from the campus. These students were not encouraged. If it were to be in the western world, I believe such students would be funded to improve on their idea and design a more acceptable station that would be of benefit to the nation.

iii. **Over-dependence on foreign goods**: It is not an exaggeration to say that Nigerians are over-dependent on foreign goods. As observed by Asoga-Allen (2001), no matter the quality of locally made goods, unless Nigerians see a stamp of Britain, USA, Japan etc. on it, they would not consider such goods to be something of value. Even though our goods or inventions are of low quality or standard, our own is our own. Those advanced countries that are producing standard goods today, passed through the same stage. There are roadside mechanics that are very knowledgeable but since they were not supported whatever good idea they have is kept with them.

iv. **Poor handling of science subjects in Nigerian schools**: This is another problem facing Nigeria in an attempt to develop scientifically and technologically. The way science subjects are handled in Nigerian schools is such that expose students to more of theoretical knowledge than practical. Most of the science students find it difficult to demonstrate what they are taught practically, and this cannot help scientific growth and development. It is not uncommon to see a Bachelor of Science (B.Sc.) degree holder in Mechanical Engineering who cannot repair a car or dismantle an engine. But talk of theory, he would tell you everything about how engine works.

v.   **Inadequate research institutions**: In Nigeria, there are not enough research institutions. Those ones that the nations have are located in the urban areas. People from the rural areas rarely have access to these research institutions. One would expect that a nation that is yearning for scientific and technological development like Nigeria would have at least a research institution in each state of the federation, but this is not so.

7.5   Suggestions towards Nigeria's Scientific Growth and Development

The following suggestions would help Nigeria to grow

scientifically and technologically:

a.   Government should give science and technology development a priority when preparing the yearly budget by allocating enough money to it;

b.   Government should be ready to fund all scientific researches in higher institutions as well as in the private sectors;

c.   The scientists should be well paid and motivated through various incentives to enable them devote much of their time to scientific investigations, which would help scientific discoveries;

d.   The talented individuals/artisans should be encouraged when they come up with any useful invention;

e.   Nigerians should develop confidence in themselves and depend less on foreigners or foreign goods because no nation can grow whether economically, scientifically or technologically, when the government and individuals lack confidence in themselves and rely on outside influence for all their needs;

f.   Science laboratories in Nigerian schools should be adequately furnished with modern facilities and science teacher should be given research allowances every month to enable them pay more attention to the teaching of science subjects in Nigeria schools/colleges;

g.   Teachers should lay more emphasis on practical than theory as this would help students to practicalise what they are taught;

h.   At least, a research institution should be built in each state of the federation to cater for research activities in that state.

Chapter Eight: Scientific Method

8.1   The Concept of Scientific Method

Scientific method refers to the processes involved in the carrying out of scientific investigation. It is the procedure or skill which is employed by the scientists in the process of solving or investigating a problem in science. The scientific method of deriving knowledge is based on the process of reflective thinking which is systematic or orderly and logical. Scientific methods followed by modern scientists include:

a.   **Identification of problems**: This is the first step in scientific process. One must identify a problem first. There are various problems facing man in man's environment. When a scientist identifies a problem, he defines the problem. This is usually done when an individual comes across a question, which gives him concern on how to derive immediate answers. Examples of such problems are: What is causing typhoid fever; why do many women die during child birth, what is bird flu? How can we prevent it? And so on and so forth

b.   **Formulation of hypothesis**: This is a process of formulating or making a tentative statement of causes or solution to a problem. The hypotheses are either proved right or wrong by the outcome of the investigation. After gathering and analysis of data, the hypothesis must be tested to determine its rightness or wrongness.

c. **Designing of instrument and collection of data**: The usual instrument used for collection of data is questionnaire. Questionnaire is designed in such a way that its reliability is guaranteed and is able to measure accurately what it is designed to measure. This is necessary because any wrongly designed questionnaire may affect the outcome of the experiment.

d. **Analysis of data collected**: This is the process of carefully analysing the data collected to see whether the outcome would provide answers to the problem being investigated.

e. **Making generalization**: This is done in science based on the outcome of the problem investigated. This can emerge in forms of laws, principles, theory etc. which become universally accepted e.g. "two parts of hydrogen and one part of oxygen makes water" is a scientific law that is the same all over the world. It has been tested, proved and verified before becoming a law.

8.2   Science and Politics

Politics has to do with ideas and activities that are concerned with the gaining and usage of power in a country, city etc. It is a profession of politicians i.e. people who seek political power in a country be it at the local, state or national level to rule others. Science, on the other hand has to do with the intellectual exercise geared towards identification of natural and artificial problems of man by diagnosing and synthesising the problems in order to discover the causes as well as the appropriate means of arresting or solving the problems.

It is important to note that both science and politics have to do with man, in the case of science, it has as its focus how to solve man's natural and artificial problems while politics has to do with how to govern the human society in order to have orderliness, and ensure that the state resources are used to the benefit of the masses and the development of the nation.

A nation that pursues scientific and technological development does so with the aim of making life conducive and worth living for its masses. For a nation to develop, politics and science must go hand in hand. Most of the facilities used in politics are the products of science. In an attempt to wipe out ignorance, diseases, poverty etc., from human society, science has to be embraced by those directing the affairs of the nation.

A technologically developed nation will be able to sustain her democracy, because there is a very likelihood that the economy of such a nation will be strong. That is, a buoyant economy is a necessary factor for a stable democracy. With a strong economy based on scientific and technological advancement, there would be job creation; citizens will be comfortable and life expectancy will be high and poverty and ignorance will be removed. Using money during elections to buy the conscience of the poor masses would disappear or be of no effect if majority of people are gainfully employed. Second-term-syndrome of political office holders will not be a do-or-die affair. Armed robbery will be minimised and territorial integrity will also be ensured when a nation is scientifically and technologically strong.

In a democratic set up, when science and technology development is put in place, mechanised agriculture is adopted to cater for food problems. Citizens are well fed and hunger is reduced if not totally eliminated. Political opportunists can no longer have their ways and victory will be based on merit.

Foreign influence on economy is likely to be removed in a democratic nation that is scientifically and technologically strong. The idea of super powers tele-guiding as to which party will rule in a country will no longer be there.

Such a technologically developed nation will be left to determine her democratic future. The economy of such a nation can no longer be controlled by the super power. There will be no master-servant relationship vis-a-vis the super powers in such a nation. A well-developed science and technology would serve as a forte or strength of democracy. Incessant change of government by "coup d'état" will be a thing of the past in a scientifically and technologically developed nation.

In most countries of the world, there are policies on science and technology. This is because the strength of a nation depends on her scientific and technological advancement. Scientists have played some roles or have a role to play in the defence of democracy. Association of Science Workers (ASW) was set up in 1933 in all parts of the world and its objective was to use science for constructive ends and like defence of democracy (UNESCO, 1979). In 1935, we had the scientists' anti-war group who were concerned with peace all over the world (UNESCO, 1979). Societies of scientists like Federation of American Scientists (FAS), British Atomic Scientists Association (BASA) had a similar objective of science for "peace around the world" all in the name of defending democracy.

The objective of science for peace is to try to stop the production of weapons and promoting science for human welfare, exchange scientific ideas and improve the teaching of science and technology. This is to improve the professionalization and economic status of workers in a democratic setup.

In summary, the importance of science to politics cannot be gainsaid. During election, there is need for effective communication, transportation, accurate data, telecommunication facilities etc. All these are products of science.

8.3   Transfer of Technology and the Third World: Myth or Reality

Transfer of technology may be defined as a process of importing machines, tools, plants, ideas and raw materials by developing nations from scientifically and technologically developed nations for use in their countries with the aid of foreign experts or expatriates who help to co-ordinate and supervise the system.

Developing nations including Nigeria in their desire to catch up with more scientifically, technologically and economically developed parts of the world import foreign technologies for production purpose. Third world countries require technology in areas such as construction of buildings, roads and dams, electricity, manufacturing of goods, transportation, communications etc. These are desirable because they are the areas of human needs.

The type of technology being transferred or allowed to be transferred by developed countries to developing countries are those that could be called "third rated technologies".

This is so because it is not a kind of technology that can make those countries to grow scientifically and technologically but only to solve their problems temporarily. For example, a situation whereby machines are imported with the expatriates to service them, the life span of such machines determines the duration of such technology. By the time all the machines are old, except new machines are imported, that may mark the end of such technology. We have seen different kinds of imported technology that did not survive the test of time due to the cost of maintaining such technologies in Nigeria.

In many parts of the country you find industries that have folded up due to one technical problem or the other or due to non-availability of spare parts. It has been so because the spare parts of the imported machines are not being manufactured in Nigeria. Rather, they are imported from countries where the machines are imported.

There is nothing to glory about in the type of technology being transferred to the third world countries. The developed countries that own the technologies are not willing to release the technical know-how or the secret of their technologies to another country. They only release what they have produced not how to produce it to the nations. If developed nations really want to help the developing nations to grow scientifically, they need to assist them on how to develop their own local technology.

It is better to teach one how to fish than to give him a fish. The foreign technologies being transferred to the third world countries are too expensive and costly to maintain, hence the need to develop local technology. Nigeria is having four refineries and none of these refineries is functioning at full capacity. They all operate below capacity. That explains why Nigeria still imports refined petrol from foreign countries to meet her local demand. Most of the time when any of these refineries breaks down, we have to spend a lot of money to bring in an expatriate to effect the repair. Also, spare parts for the refineries are imported from abroad. This is so because the third-rated technologies imported massively by developing countries have little or no facilities for spare parts manufacture locally, and require specific engineers not only to install them, but also to repair them when faulty, at great cost to the importing countries. With that, they become more of a problem.

In the light of the above, it should be realised that technology transfer is a ruse. It exist only in the realm of deception and a form of neo-colonialism. This is not to say that few of such imported technologies have not survived in Nigeria and other developing countries of the world. However, the very few that have survived have constrained the movement towards technological progress and achievement of maximum production. Other reasons for lack of technological growth range from mass illiteracy and scarcity of indigenous industrial and managerial skills, shortage of capital, heavy dependence on foreign source for plant and machinery, to inflation which increases costs of production and development projects. Not to be left out are unfavourable fiscal policies, trade and foreign exchange restrictions, bureaucratic red tape, unnecessary delay and inefficient infrastructural facilities.

In conclusion, the developed countries should help the developing countries to generate their own indigenous technology geared towards solving their own social problems instead of using the developing countries as a dumping ground for their technological products called transfer of technology.

8.4   Revision Questions

a.   Define the term "scientific methods"

b.   Discuss in detail scientific methods or processes

c.   Science and politics have roles to play in human society. Discuss

d.   Is there any relationship between science and politics?

e.   What do you understand by transfer of technology?

f.   Attempt an appraisal of technological transfer from the developed countries to the developing countries

g.   How real is the issue of technological transfer from the developed countries to the Third World countries?

Chapter Nine: The Computer and Developing Nations

9.1 The Concept of Computer

Computer is a programmable machine that can store, retrieve and process information or data for educational use, scientific research work, business and other purposes. Its origin the "Abacus" was invented by the Chinese in 400 BC. The first electronic computer was produced by Charles Babbage's assisted by Ada, the Countess of Lovelace and daughter of Lord Byron (Moursund, 1992).

Computer is made up of interrelated set of components working together as a unit. The main components are:

☐ **Input Device**: This enables the user to feed information into the computer. The feeding or input may be done by means of teletype, punch card, magnetic tape or other devices.

☐ **Output Device**: The Cathode Ray Tube (CRT) and the various printing devices that produce hard copies of the processed input

☐ **Disk Drive Unit**: The disk drive is used to read or write data onto one or more diskettes.

☐ **Main Memory**: The main memory of the computer brain is the system that stores information for later retrieval. Examples are the Random Access Memory (RAM) and Read Only Memory (ROM). It also stores the arithmetic operations received from "ALU" and supplies information to the output unit.

☐ **Computer Hardware**: The tangible physical components of a computer system.

☐ **Computer Software**: The tasks e.g. instructions in programs that make computer perform particular function. These programs are written in language or code which can be interpreted by the computer.

9.2. Functions of a Computer

A computer processes information known as data. Among other things, a computer performs the following functions:

i. It accepts data
ii. It processes data
iii. It supplies data often referred to as an output
iv. It stores data.

Other machines that can be used to process data

include the adding machine, the slide rule etc. What actually distinguish a computer from other machines is speed, capacity and versatility.

9.3.   Classifications of Computer

Basically, computer can be classified into three main classes. These include:

The mainframe computer

The microcomputer and

The mini-computer

The Mainframe Computer

The mainframe computer is the largest among the three classes of computers. It is found in computer rooms of corporations, financial institutions, universities and business companies. The mainframe computers provide the capability to execute applications requiring large amount of data. It has great speed, greater memory and external storage than the other two types, and it is capable of serving many computer terminals at one time.

The Microcomputer

It is a computer based on large scale integration that is physically very small and can be placed on a desk. It provides more employment opportunities to users than mainframe.

The Mini-Computer

This is smaller than the mainframe computer and larger than the microcomputer. It has less computing power than the mainframe computer and it also requires less attendant staff. It is used for a wide range of commercial and scientific applications.

9.4   Importance of Computer to Education

Computer can be programmed:

- ☐ To present visual and audio materials to the learners.
- ☐ To analyse their response.
- ☐ To make a diagnosis of their difficulties.
- ☐ To select the most appropriate material and mode of presentation for learner's assignment.
- ☐ To be used as a test scoring machine.
- ☐ To be used for record keeping.
- ☐ To be used for monitoring the progress of the learner
- ☐ Computer can be used as self-contained unit for individualised instruction

Throughout the world, people are now aware of the importance of computer. In developing country like

Nigeria, there is massive rush for computer education in order to become computer literate. The awareness has been created, people are now conscious of the fact that whatever is one's field of specialisation, the knowledge of computer is a must in modern time. A lot of people are now computer literate. It is the social demand of the new millennium. Some employers especially in the private sector require the knowledge of computer from whoever wants to join them

9.4   Revision Questions

1.   What is computer?
2.   Mention the various components of computer
3.   What are the functions of computer?
4.   Discuss the classes of computer
5.   State the importance of computer to education

Chapter Ten: Mechanisation of Agriculture

10.1 The Concept of Mechanisation of Agriculture

Mechanisation of Agriculture is the application of modern technology to agriculture in order to enhance mass production of agricultural produce. Before the advent of modern technology, the equipment used by peasant farmers include cutlass, hoe, diggers etc. Farming at that period required hard labour and it was characterised by low productivity. The output of labour is very low due to crude implements being used.

With the discovery of modern technology, machines are now used to do most of the works done by men and this has made it possible for farming to be carried out on a large scale thereby leading to mass production of agricultural produce. In mechanisation of agriculture, most of the work is done by machines while men only operate the machines and repair. The mechanisation of agriculture brings about greater efficiency because the machine e.g. a tractor, could cultivate in a day the land that would have been cultivated by 50 men or more in two days.

Nigeria like many other African countries is greatly

endowed with excellent climatic conditions, fertile land and varieties of cultivable crops. According to Ekemode, Arabami and Sanbe (2000), the country occupies a land mass of 98 million hectares of land which 75 percent represents five (5) ecological zones suitable for agriculture, including arable farming, forestry, livestock, and fisheries. They said further, that in spite of all these rich endowments, recent surveys indicate that over 70 percent of Nigerians are living below the poverty line with the incidence of malnutrition increasing daily as witnessed by the sharp decline of per capita income.

The vast fertile land of Nigeria is yet to be utilised for agricultural development by using mechanised system. Farming in Nigeria today is still in the hand of poor peasant farmers who cannot afford mechanisation of agriculture. Majority of these peasant farmers produce for consumption with little or nothing to sell.

It is a fact that mechanised agriculture is in itself an industry that is capable of employing all the jobless graduates and school leavers in Nigeria. But much has not been done in this direction. In developed countries like America, Britain, etc., a lot of people are into agriculture. This is so because agriculture has been mechanised in these countries and there are storage facilities for agricultural produce. Farmers are very rich in developed countries unlike the situation in developing countries where agriculture is not mechanised.

10.2   Problems Facing Mechanisation of Agriculture in Nigeria

There are numerous problems facing mechanisation of agriculture in Nigeria. These include:

a.   Land ownership system.

b.   High cost of mechanical agricultural equipment.

c.   Lack of preservation or storage facilities.

d.   Neglect of agriculture.

e.   Lack of social amenities in rural areas.

f.   Over-dependence on crude oil.

g.   Lack of encouragement to the farmers.

h.   Wrong mentality towards farming

i.   Lack of indigenous technology

a.   **Land Ownership System**: This is one of the problems of mechanisation of agriculture in Nigeria because lands are owned by individuals or families. No one has right to interfere or trespass into another person's land. Most communities only lend out land for a period of time and take it back at the expiration of the contract. In short, it is difficult to obtain land for the development of mechanised agriculture that requires heavy investment.

b.   **High cost of mechanical agricultural equipment**: The equipment needed for mechanised agriculture requires a lot of capital. Most private farmers are far from being able to afford such equipment. Where such types of equipment are procured, there is need for maintenance. Those who would have loved to go into mechanised farming lack the means.

c.   **Lack of preservation or storage facilities**: Nigeria is yet to develop sufficiently the technology on storage or preservation of farm or agricultural produce. This has made it impossible for farmers to store surplus produce during harvest period for future sales. Thus, the farmers are forced by necessity to turn out all their produce at the same time and, at a cheaper rate. Unlike the situation in advanced or developed countries where you can get a particular agricultural produce to buy throughout the year. In Nigeria, one can only get a particular farm produce at a particular season and after that season, they become scarce.

Storage facilities would make it possible for farmers to get better prices for their produce. Lack of storage facilities is one of the major reasons why farmers in Nigeria are poor.

d.   **Neglect of agriculture**: Agriculture has been neglected in Nigeria because of the oil boom. Unfortunately, the oil boom has not brought about the desired development to the polity because of corruption and extravagance of those in government. Before the discovery of crude oil in Nigeria, the country was already doing well in international trade. The nation's major export commodities then were cocoa, palm oil, coffee, rubber, etc. But with the advent of crude oil, the cultivation of these commodities gradually died off. This happened because people now look at farming as a dirty job, more so as it involves a lot of labour.

e.   **Lack of social amenities in rural areas**: In most rural areas of Nigeria, there are no good roads, not to talk of electricity and pipe-borne water. This has made people to develop great desire for living in the urban areas where these facilities or amenities are found. The urban cities are crowded because of rural-urban drift but farm lands are scarce in urban areas. It is a serious problem that requires urgent attention if people who are supposed to work and produce food for the nation continue to move to the urban in search of office work.

f.   **Over-dependence on crude oil**: The government and people of Nigeria have over-depended on crude oil as the main source of income. And this is not good enough because oil will dry up one day. The agricultural sector is supposed to be developed alongside crude oil exploitation. It is not proper for a country that is blessed with fertile land like Nigeria to be importing food from other countries, when it is possible for us to be a food-exporting nation.

g.   **Lack of encouragement to the farmers**: In Nigeria, farmers are not given enough encouragement. The farmers need money to expand their farmland and increase their production. In most cases when farmers are given loans by the government, they rarely harvest their produce before such loans are collected back from them. There should be enough time for them to repay such loans that would help them to re-invest in their farmland. Even where government purchase some equipment to be rented out to farmers, the amount required for such rent is out of reach for the poor peasant farmers.

h.   **Wrong mentality towards farming**: There is wrong mentality among majority of Nigerians that farming is a dirty job. People seem not to believe that they can make it through farming or agriculture because, most of our farmers are poor and farming with crude implement makes one grow old quickly.

i.   **Lack of indigenous technology**: Nigeria is yet to develop any meaningful technology in agriculture. All the needed equipment for mechanised agriculture are still being imported from the developed countries including spare parts.   The worst part is that the maintenance or repair aspect has to be done by experts from the country of export which makes it expensive and unsuitable for the developing nation like Nigeria

10.3   Suggestions towards Overcoming the Problems Facing Mechanisation of Agriculture in Nigeria

The following suggestions would help in alleviating the problems facing mechanisation of agriculture in Nigeria. These include:

a.   Government should acquire unused lands and make them available for genuine farmers for farming.

b.   Government should import mechanical agriculture equipment and make them available to farmers at cheap rate to enable all farmers to make use of them.

c.   Nigerian scientists should wake up from their slumber and come up with local storage facilities or preservation technology that can be used by farmers to preserve their produce after harvest to prevent wastages.

d.   Government, at all levels, should set the pace by going into an extensive mechanised agriculture. This would help to solve a lot of problems facing the nation and make life conducive for the generality of the people.

e.   Rural communities should be provided with social amenities to enable people stay there and concentrate on farming and stop rural-urban drift. This is necessary because, a lot of people who would have made their fortune through farming are roaming the urban cities looking for unavailable jobs.

f.   The agricultural sector should be developed and promoted because food is very important for human existence, and when food is out of poverty, there is no doubt that poverty is minimised.

g.   Agricultural development banks should be resuscitated to give loans to farmers at low interest, and reasonable period of time for repayment should be allowed so as to enhance their productivity.

h.   Agriculture experts should be given loans to go

into farming in their field of specialisation. This would alleviate the problem of agriculture graduates looking for office job.

10.4   Prospects of Mechanisation of Agriculture in Nigeria

There is no doubt that agriculture is a traditional and first occupation of man. Mechanisation of agriculture is capable of transforming the economy of a nation from a poor one to a buoyant and formidable economy. Ekemode, Arabami and Sanbe (2000) outlined 13 importance of agriculture to Nigeria economy. These include:

a.   Provision of food for the teeming population;

b.   Provision of employment for the populace;

c.   Provision of income for farmers and workers engaged in agriculture;

d.   Provision of raw material for industries;

e.   Provision of materials for shelter;

f.   Provision of materials for clothing;

g.   Source of foreign exchange for the country;

h.   Provision of facilities for recreation and tourism;

i.   Promotion of diplomatic and international relations;

j.   Provision of market for industrial goods;

k.   Provision of herbs used for medicinal purposes;

l. Promotion of culture and traditions;

m. Contribution to the field of education for manpower development.

Despite all the problems facing mechanisation of agriculture in Nigeria, it is hoped that the future of mechanised agriculture is bright, more so if there is a civilian government that is interested in putting agriculture in place. The existing organisations/institutions such as River Basin Development Authorities, Agriculture and Cooperative Banks etc. should be re-organised to make them alive to their responsibilities. It is hoped that the step being taken by one civilian government would be followed by the successive governments in future.

In addition, the various fertilizer companies springing up in various parts of Nigeria would also help to boost food production and farming in Nigeria. The prices of agricultural produce have appreciated, farmers are now becoming rich. This is an incentive and motivation to Nigerian farmers. Lastly, centres for seed multiplication scheme have been created by government for improved animal and fish product programmes, and improved breeding of livestock and poultry.

10.5 Revision Questions

a. Give clear definition of mechanisation of agriculture.

b. Discuss the obstacles to mechanisation of agriculture in Nigeria.

c. Suggest means by which problems facing mechanisation of agriculture could be solved in Nigeria.

d. What are the prospects of mechanisation of agriculture in Nigeria?

Chapter Eleven: Traditional Science

11.1 The Concept of Traditional Science

Before modern science and technology was introduced by the white men, there had been science and technology in Africa. People have various ways through which they solved their natural and artificial problems. People arrived at these various means through what could be regarded as primitive intellectual activities, though the means employed by people in getting their solutions were not the same with that of modern science in terms of empiricism, for not all the discoveries or ideas are provable.

That notwithstanding, people engage in serious thinking, identified problems and through trial and error, arrived at solution to some identified problems. These activities of our fore fathers are regarded as traditional science because science is an intellectual activity that tends to make life conducive for man. These activities to a large extent help to solve some of the problems facing man in the environment.

Tradition has to do with existing culture, ideas and beliefs developed by a group of people which has become part and parcel of them over a long period of time. Traditional science therefore, can be defined as the intellectual activities developed by the primitive people for solving their problems before the advent of modern science and technology. The activities of man in traditional society geared towards solving his problems cut across all spheres of human life. For example, traditional science is felt in the areas like transportation, communication, health, agriculture, etc.

It is important to note that some of the means employed in traditional society to solve man's problems are unscientific, rather, it has to do with beliefs in magic, witchcraft and superstitions. All these are not open to rational examination or proof. People studied their environment and discovered that certain animals, plants, trees have certain powers which are capable of healing certain diseases in man.

11.2   Scope of Traditional Science

Traditional science is applied to all realms of man's life and problems. The most tangible areas of coverage include agriculture, transportation, communication, health, engineering etc. How traditional science affects the above-mentioned areas shall be discussed in detail in this chapter.

11.3   How Traditional Science Affects Agriculture

Agriculture is undoubtedly the first occupation of the early man. Man learned to know when to plant at a particular time of the year through intellectual study of the weather and the environment. The type of crops for rainy season will never be planted in dry season. Also, the number of months required for each crop to mature for harvest was discovered.

The tools needed for farming were invented by the people, such tools included, cutlass, hoes etc. Apart from the sound knowledge of when to plant, the people believed that gods had to be consulted before any planting could take place. To cultivate a large piece of land, people form themselves into groups that work for one another to make their work easy and quick.

A group may consist of ten members or more. If they work in Kunle's farm today, tomorrow they move to Ojo's farm. They continue with this until the last person's farm is worked upon. This method helps the individual farmer to expand his farm holding for the year. Because, where ten persons work in a day, a single person may not be able to cover it in fourteen days; this is due to the joint effort used to accomplish such work.

The traditional people do not make use of fertilizer but

adopt a farming system known as shifting cultivation. Shifting cultivation is a process whereby a parcel of land is cultivated for a year and after harvest the farmer moves to another land in order to allow the previous land to regain its fertility.

After harvest, some crops are preserved using local technology. For example, maize bunches are usually hung on the roof of the tent at kitchen where smoke from the fire can prevent any insect from entering it. Likewise, fish or meat is usually dried with the fire and later kept in a pot hanged very close to the smoke of fire in the kitchen. This is to prevent such from getting spoilt and to preserve same for days, weeks or months.

The harvested crops are processed in most cases. For example, cassava may be turned to gari and fufu; yam to pounded yam; maize to a type of food Yoruba people called ogi or eko, etc. In some communities before harvest, gods has to be consulted and the best crop in the farm has to be sacrificed to gods. The belief is that this would ensure bumper harvest in the next farming season.

11.4   How Traditional Science Affects Transportation

Transportation is the movement of goods and passengers from one place to the other. Before cars, motorcycles and others were invented, people in the traditional society had one way or the other of transporting themselves and their goods from one place to the other. These are some of the ways by which people transported themselves:

a. **By Trekking**: People may trek a long distance which may take them days before arriving at their destinations. With trekking, the magnitude of load or good carried depended on the strength of the person carrying it. In essence, much load could not be carried through this means. Trekking is labour intensive and it weakens the body.

b. **By using horses, camels and donkeys**: In most parts of Africa where these animals are found, they are used for transportation. They carry persons and goods. These animals can travel a long distance without food. They help the farmers to transport their farm produce to the market or home. Though, not as fast as cars or motorcycles, these animals make the journey faster and easier than trekking.

c. **Through mysterious ways**: It is believed that our forefathers made most of their long journeys in the past through mysterious power. After reciting the required incantation, they would find themselves in the place where they want to be immediately. This process is even faster than aeroplane but the problem with this system is that it cannot be proved scientifically. However, evidence abounds that it existed in those days. Among the Yorubas, this is called ofe or kanako

11.5 How Traditional Science Affects Communication

Communication is a means whereby messages are sent and received. In traditional African society, there are various ways of sending and receiving messages. At the town level when there is a message to be passed to the people, the town crier is sent. The town crier always hold in his hand a gong, which he beats with an iron rod momentarily to arrest people's attention. It is customary for people to listen and suspend whatever they are doing when they hear the sound. Such message usually emanate from the king or a highly placed member of the society.

Sometimes, trumpet may be used. Talking drum is another means of communication among people who speak the same language. This is common among the Yoruba people of Nigeria. Experts in drumming handles talking drum and pass message to the people.

Talking drum can be used to praise people, reprimand, and caution or humiliate, depending on the message the drummer intends to pass. Another means of traditional communication is through body signs. Without opening mouth to talk, people can pass message to each other through the use of body signs. It may be through the use of hands, head, leg, stomach, eyes, etc. This is common within people of the same culture and language.

Another means of communication is through the making of certain customary sounds. For example, two people working in different parts of the bush can communicate with each other through the use of certain customary sounds. When the first person makes the sound, the second person who understands the sound would respond in a correct fashion to the sound. This method can be used to greet each other, or tell each other farewell, etc.

Weeds or branches of trees can also be used to communicate or pass message. For example, two people who pass the same route to the farm or village market can use this means. When the first one to get to the junction wants to tell the one behind that he has passed, he may tie some weeds together at the top or hold a branch of a tree and tie some leaves together. When the one behind sees this, he would easily understand that his friend or brother, sister has gone before him.

An object may be sent by an Oba to another Oba and as soon as he receives it, the message is understood. This is called *Aroko* in Yorubaland. Secret messages are usually sent through this means. The person sent on such message cannot know the meaning except the person who the message is meant for. The message may even be about the person sent on that message.

11.6   How Traditional Science Affects Health

In traditional African society, people believe that good health is the back bone of wealth. A person that is sick cannot talk of wealth. Good health is likened to peace, which people believe is above all things. It is generally believed in the traditional society that God created trees, leaves, herbs and animals, for use of man. Not only does man use these things for food but also for curing various ailments and diseases in man. The farmers and the hunters spend most of their time in the forest and as a result of regular contact and experimentation through trial and error methods; they discover those that are suitable for curing specific diseases.

Ever before the advent of orthodox medicine, people in the traditional society have been using leaves, herbs, trees to cure diseases like malaria fever, stomach trouble, eye problem, itching etc. Traditional science as it relates to health goes beyond using of herbs and roots for curing alone; it also has to do with mysterious power. For example, among the Ijaw community, people specialises in the setting of bones when one sustains a fracture. The process looks somehow mysterious. Before treatment starts, a fowl leg will be broken. As the person with fracture is being treated and the fowl leg is healing up, the fracture also will be healing. When the fowl has fully recovered, the person with fracture will feel no pain again.

Another mysterious way of healing sickness is to consult the Ifa oracle. Through Ifa Priest, oracle would make it known if the sickness is caused by any wrongdoing or offence committed by the sick person or it is an affliction of the enemy on the person. Whichever way, Ifa oracle would prescribe the type of sacrifice to make and the type of animal to be used for the sacrifice. When the sacrifice is made, the person will be healed. This mysterious healing is common in all African societies and it has to do with the belief in witchcraft, gods and superstitions.

As important as traditional science on health is,

researches have been and are being carried out at the national and international levels on how to incorporate traditional medicine into orthodox medicine. It is not an exaggeration to say that traditional medicine is found to be more effective in healing certain diseases or ailments. Fracture is a good example. In an orthodox medicine, anybody with serious fracture would have to be amputated, but with traditional medicine, no matter the magnitude of such fracture, once the pieces of the bone could be extracted, it would be joined together and the person would become whole. There are others e.g. pile, hitching, etc that traditional medicine is highly effective in healing.

11.7   How Traditional Science Affects Defence

This has to do with the way people defend themselves and territory against enemies and external attack using traditional science.

This is usually done physically and spiritually. Physically, people train their young ones to be physically strong. This is done through various exercises e.g. wrestling, boxing, tug of war, weightlifting etc. In addition to this, people engage in manufacturing of concrete objects e.g. bludgeon, stones, and others which they used on their opponents whenever there is war or confrontation.

Spiritually, people make use of charm, amulet,

incantations etc. when fighting wars. Though, this may look mysterious and empirical but it is real. Some of those who believe in these are really very strong. When you shoot some of them with modern weapon, it may not penetrate their bodies. Mere beating somebody who has juju against such may result in the death of the person that beat him except the person too is strong in juju.

11.8   How Traditional Science Affects Engineering

Apart from fashioning tools in a local way, traditional science is used to build traditional houses. In those days, people built houses made of mud, bamboo pole, etc. Roofing is usually done with palm leaves and weeds. In most rural areas, because people cannot afford the cost of modern houses, traditional houses are still in vogue. In the riverine areas, people erect planks above the water level and build their houses on it. Planks are used for such building and palm leaves are used for roofing.

In order to enjoy cold water during afternoon when it is hot, people build a pot which is partly below the earth level with a cover. This is used for storing water. Water from such pots is usually cold anytime of the day. This serves as local refrigerator. People make use of calabash plates for eating, and calabash trays for carrying loads from the farm or to the market.

In conclusion, traditional science served the local and primitive society before the advent of science and technology civilization. Though, traditional science is not completely out of place today as it still exists in alongside modern science especially in the rural African communities, and it is still being used in the area of health, defence, communication, to mention a few.

Chapter Twelve: Marginalization

12.1   Meaning of Marginalization

Marginalization is the social process of becoming or being made marginal (to relegate or confine to a lower social standing or outer limit or edge, as of social standing); "the marginalization of the underclass", "marginalization of the minority group" and many others are some examples. Marginalization involves people being denied degree of power, importance, rights and privileges. Marginalization has the potential to result in severe material deprivation, and its most extreme form can exterminate groups, (mullary, 2007).

Material deprivation is the most common result of marginalization when looking at how unfairly material resources such as food and shelter are dispersed in the society. Along with material deprivation, marginalised individuals are also excluded from services, programs and policies (Young, 2000). Marginalization can be understood within three levels: - individual, community and global structural policies. Although examples are listed within these three specific levels, one must recognise the interesting nature of marginalization and its capacity to overlap within each individual

Marginalization at the individual level results in an individual's exclusion from meaningful exclusion in society. An example of marginalization at the individual level is the exclusion of single mother from the welfare system prior to the welfare reform of the 1900s. The welfare system is based on the concept of the universal worker; entitlement to welfare based on one's contribution to the society in form of employment. A single mother's contribution to society is not based on employment resulting in the mother's intelligibility of social assistance for many decades. In modern society caring more is devalued and motherhood is seen as a barrier to employment (Lessa 2006).

Single mothers are marginalised for their significant role in the socializing of children and due to views that an individual can only contribute meaningfully to society through employment. As a result, single mothers continue to suffer from material deprivation as well as their children (Lessa 2006).

Another example of individual marginalization is seen in the exclusion of individuals with disabilities from the labour force. Grandz (as cited in Leslie 2003) discusses an employer viewpoint in hiring individuals living with disabilities as jeopardizing [productivity, increasing the rate of absenteeism and creating more accidents in the work place cant or (as cited in Leslie 2003) also discusses as employers concern of the excessive high cost of accommodating people with disabilities.

The marginalization of individuals with disabilities is prevalent today despite the Canadian Human Rights Act, the employment equity act, academic achievement, skills and training (Leslie, 2003).

12.2   Community

Many communities experience marginalisation, with particular focus in the section on the aboriginal communities and women. Marginalization of aboriginal communities is a product of colonialisms, aboriginal communities lost their land were forced into destitute areas, lost their sources of income and was excluded from the labour market.   Additionally, communities lost their culture and values through forced assimilation and lost their rights in society (Baskin, 2003). Today various communities continue to be marginalised from society due to the development of practices, [policies and programs that "met the needs of Bourgeoisies and not the needs of marginalised groups themselves" (Yee 2005). He also connects marginalisation to minority communities when describing the concept of whiteness as maintaining and enforcing developmental norms and discourse. A typical example of marginalized group and communities in Nigeria are the Niger Delta people and their communities. The Niger Delta areas form the economic life-wire of Nigeria due to the discovery of crude oil in the area as far back as 1959, and since the exploitation of this resources, the people of the area were not catered for in any scheme of things, the income from the crude oil were spent to develop the towns and villages of those ruling the nation. The Niger-Deltans grown under bondage of poverty, neglect and environmental degradation. Marginalization of community and its people have negative implication especially when the marginalized group acquire strength or secure the backing of sponsors. Sponsors here may be well to do individuals or nations. For example, the marginalization of the Niger Deltans have led to the emergence of militant groups in the area who kill, maim, kidnap and commit all sorts of atrocities in Nigeria. If a situation like that is not properly handled, it may result in a full blown war that can destabilize the nation and cause lost of lives and properties.

A second example of marginalization at the community level is the marginalization of women. Moosa-mitha (as cited in Brown and Strega, 2005) discuss the feminist movement as a direct reaction to the marginalisation of women in society. In some communities and cultures women were excluded from the labour force and their working in the home was not valued, feminists argued that men and women should equally participate in the labour force, the public and private sector, and in the home. They also focused on labour laws to increase access to employment, as well as recognize child rearing as a valuable form of labour.

Today's women are still marginalized from executive positions and continue to earn less than men in upper management positions.

12.3   Conflict in the Niger Delta

The current conflict in the Niger-Delta arose in the early 1930's due to tensions between the foreign oil corporations and a number of the Niger Delta's minority ethnic groups who felt they were being exploited particularly the ogoni and the ijaw. Ethnic and the political unrest have continued throughout the 1990's and persist as of 2007 despite the conversion to democracy and the election of the Obasanjo government in 1999. Competition for oil wealth has fuelled violence between innumerable ethnic groups, causing the militarization of nearly the entire region by ethnic militia group as well as Nigerian military and police forces (notably the Nigerian Mobile Police).

Victims of crimes are fearful of seeking justice for crimes committed against them because of growing impurity from prosecution for individuals responsible for serious human rights abuses (which) has created a devastating cycle of increasing conflict and violence. The regional and ethnic conflicts are so numerous that fully detailing each is impossible and impractical. However, there have been a number of major confrontations that deserve elaborations

12.4 Background to the Conflict

Nigeria after nearly four decades of oil production had by the early 1990s become almost completely dependent on petroleum extraction economically, generating 25% of its GDP (this has since risen to 40% as of 2000). Despite the vast wealth created by petroleum, the benefit has been slow to trickle down to the majority of the population, who since the 1960s have increasingly been forced to abandon their traditional agricultural practices. Annual production of both cash and food crops dropped significantly in the later decades of 20th century, cocoa production dropped by 43% (Nigeria was the world's largest cocoa exporter in 1960), rubber dropped by 29%, cotton by 65% and groundnut by 64%. In spite of the large number of skilled well-paid Nigerians who have been employed by the oil corporations, the majority of Nigerians and most especially the Niger-Delta states and the far north have become poorer since the 1960s.

The Delta region has a steadily growing population estimated to be over 30 million people as of 2005, accounting for more than 23% of Nigerian's total population. The population density is also among the highest in the world with 265 people per kilometre squared. This population is expanding at a rapid, 3% per year and the oil capital, Port Harcourt along with other large towns are growing quickly. Poverty and urbanization in Nigeria are on the rise and official corruption is considered a fact of life. The resultant scenario is one in which there is urbanisation but no accompanying economic growth to provide jobs. This has led to a section of the growing populace assisting in destroying the ecosystem that they require to sustain themselves.

12.5   The Case of Ogoniland (1992-1995)

Ogoniland is a 404 square-mile (1,050km) region in the southeast of the Niger Delta Basin. Economically viable petroleum was discovered in Ogoniland in 1957, just one year after the discovery of Niger as first commercial petroleum deposit, with Royal Dutch Shell and Chevron Corporation setting up shop throughout the next two decades. The Ogoni people are minority ethnic group with a population of about half a million, and other ethnic groups in the region attest that during this time, the government began forcing them to abandon their land to oil companies without consultation and offering tangible and life sustaining compensation. This is further supported by 1979 Constitutional addition which afforded the Federal Government full ownership and rights to all Nigerian territory and also decided that all compensation for land would "be based on the value of the crops on the land at the time of its acquisition, not on the value of the land itself." The Nigerian government could now distribute the land to oil companies as it deem fit

The 1970s and 1980s saw the government empty promises of benefits for the Niger-Delta peoples fall through, with the Ogoni growing increasing dissatisfied and their environmental, social, and economic apparatus rapidly deteriorating. The Movement for the Survival of the Ogoni People (MOSOP) was formed in 1992. MOSOP, spearheaded by Ogoni playwright and author Ken Saro-Wiwa, became the major campaigning organization representing the Ogoni people in the struggle for ethnic and environmental rights. Its primary targets, and at times adversaries, have been the Nigerian government and Royal Dutch Shell.

Beginning in December 1992, the conflict between Ogoni and the oil infrastructure escalated to a level of greater seriousness and intensity on both sides. Both parties began carrying out acts of violence and MOSOP issued an ultimatum to the oil companies (Shell, Chevron and the Nigerian National Petroleum Corporation) which demanded some $10 billion in accumulated royalties, damages and compensation, and "immediate stoppage of environmental degradation", and negotiations for mutual agreement on all future drilling.

The Ogonis threatened to embark on mass action to disrupt their operation if the companies failed to comply. By this act, the Ogoni shifted the focus of their actions from an unresponsive federal government to the oil companies engaged in their own region. The rationale for this assignment of responsibility was the benefits accrued by the oil companies from extracting the natural wealth of the Ogoni homeland, and neglect from central government.

The government responded by banning public gatherings and declaring that disturbances of oil production were acts of treason. Oil extraction from the territory had slowed to a trickle of 10,000 barrels per day (5% of the national total).

Military repression escalated in May 1994. On May 21, Soldiers and mobile policemen appeared in most Ogoni villages. On that day, four Ogoni chiefs (all on the conservative side of a schism within MOSOP over strategy) were brutally murdered. Saro-Wiwa, head of the opposing faction, had been denied entry to Ogoni land on the day of the murders, but he was detained in connection with the killings. The occupying forces, led by Major Paul Okuntimo of Rivers State Internal Security, claimed to be searching for those directly responsible for the killings of the four Ogonis. However, witnesses say that they engaged in terror operations against the general Ogoni population. Amnesty International characterized the policy as deliberate terrorism. By mid-June, the security forces had razed 30 villages, detained 600 people and killed at least 40. The figure eventually rose to 2,000 civilian deaths and the displacement of around 100,000 internal refugees.

In May 1994, nine activists from the movement who would become known as 'The Ogoni Nine' among them [Ken Saro-Wiwa, were arrested and accused of incitement to murder following the deaths of four Ogoni elders. Saro-Wiwa and his comrades denied the charges, but were imprisoned for over a year before being found guilty and sentenced to death by a specially convened tribunal, hand-selected by General Sanni Abacha on 10 November 1995. The activists were denied due process and upon being found guilty, were hanged by the Nigerian state.

The executions were met with an immediate international response. The trial was widely criticised by human right organizations soldiers, three more protesters were shot dead including Nwashuku Okeri and Ghadafi Ezeifile. The military declared a state of emergency throughout Bayelsa state, imposed a dusk-to-dawn curfew, and banned meetings. At military roadblocks, local residents were severely beaten or detained. At night, soldiers invaded private homes, terrorizing residents with beatings and women and girls with rape.

On January 4, 1999 about 100 soldiers from military base at Chevron's Escravos facility attacked Opia and Ikiyan, two Ijaw communities in Delta state. Bright

Pablogba, the traditional leader of Ikiyan, who came to the river to negotiate with the soldiers, was shot along with a seven-year-old girl and possibly dozens of others. Of the approximately 1,000 people living in the two villages, four people were found dead and sixty-two were still missing months after the attack. The same soldiers set the villages ablaze, destroy canoes and fishing equipment, killed livestock, and destroyed churches and religious shrines.

Nonetheless, Operation Climate Change continued, and disrupted Nigerian oil supplies through much of 1999 by turning off valves through Ijaw territory. In the context of high conflict between the Ijaw and the Nigerian Federal Government (and its police and army), the military carried out Odi massacre, killing scores if not hundreds of Ijaws.

Subsequent actions by Ijaws against the oil industry included both renewed efforts at nonviolent action and militarized attacks on foreign oil workers.

12.6　The Creation of the Niger Delta Development Commission (2000)

The Niger Delta Development Commission (NDDC) was established by President Olusegun Obasanjo with the sole mandate of developing the oil-rich Niger-Delta region of southern Nigeria. Since its inauguration, the NDDC has focused on the development of social and physical infrastructures, ecological/environmental remediation and human development. A new ministry called Niger Delta Ministry was created in 2008, to address the Niger-Delta issue by President Umaru Musa Yaradua), but most Niger Deltans see it as a distraction from the federal government since they also have the Niger Delta Development Commission in place too.

12.7   The Emergence of Armed Groups in the Delta Region (2003 - 2004)

The ethnic unrest and conflicts in the late 1990s (such as those between Ijaw and Itshekiri) coupled with a spike in the availability of small arms and other weapons, led increasingly to the militarization of the Delta. By this time, local and state officials had become involved by offering financial support to those paramilitary groups they believed would attempt to enforce their own political agenda. Conflagrations have been concentrated primarily in Delta and Rivers states.

Prior to 2003, the epicentre of regional violence was Warri. However, after the violence convergence of the

largest military groups in the region, the Niger Delta
Peoples Volunteer Force (NDPVF) led by Mujahid
Dokubo-Asari and the Niger Delta Vigilante (NDV)
led by Ateke Tom (both of which are comprised
primarily of Ijaws), conflict became focused on Port
Harcourt and outlying towns. The two groups dwarf a
plethora of smaller militias supposedly numbering
more than one hundred. The Nigerian government
classified these groups as "cults", many of which
began as local university fraternities. The groups have
adopted names largely based on Western culture, some
of which include Icelanders, Greenlanders, KKK, and
Vultures. All of the groups are constituted mostly by
disaffected young men from Warri, Port Harcourt, and
their sub-urban areas. Although the smaller groups are
autonomous from within, they have formed alliances
with and are largely controlled from above by either
Asari and his NDPDF or Tom's NDV who provided
military support and instruction.

The NDPVF which was founded by Asari, a former
president of Ijaw Youth Council, in 2003 after he
"retreated into the bush" to form the group with the
explicit goal of acquiring control of regional petroleum
resources. The NDPVF attempted to control such
resources primarily through oil "bunkering", a process
in which an oil pipeline is tapped and the oil extracted
onto a barge. Oil corporations and the Nigerian state

point out that bunkering is illegal; militant justify bunkering, saying they are being exploited and have not received adequate profits from profitable but ecologically destructive oil industry. Bunkered oil can be sold for profit, usually to destinations in West Africa, but also abroad. Bunkering is a fairly common practice in the Delta but in this case the militia groups are the primary perpetrators.

The intense confrontation between the NDPVF and NDV seems to have been brought about by Asari's political falling out with the NDPVF's financial supporter Peter Odili, governor of River State following the April 2003 local and state elections. After Asari publicly criticized the election process as fraudulent, the Odili government withdrew its financial support from the NDPVF and began to support Tom's NDV, effectively launching a paramilitary campaign against the NDPVF.

Subsequent violence occurred chiefly in riverine villages southeast and southwest of Port Harcourt, with two groups fighting and the government of other states, who condemned the Nigerian government's long history of detaining their critics, mainly pro-democracy and other political activists. The Commonwealth of Nations, which has also pleaded for clemency, suspended Nigerian membership in response. The United States, The United Kingdom and European Union (EU) all implemented sanctions, but not on petroleum (Nigeria's main export).

Shell claims it asked the Nigerian government for clemency towards those found guilty, but its request was refused. However, a 2001 Greenpeace report found that "two witnesses that accused them [Saro-Wiwa and other activists] later admitted that Shell and the military had bribed them with promises of money and jobs at Shell. Shell admitted having given money to the Nigerian military, who brutally tried to silence the voices which claimed justice.

As of 2006, the situation in Ogoniland has eased significantly assisted by the transition to the democratic rule in 1999. However, no attempts have been made by the government or an international body to bring about justice by investigating and prosecuting those involved in the violence and property destruction that have occurred in Ogoniland, although a class action law suit was brought against Shell by individual plaintiffs in the US.

REFERENCES

Abraham, J. A. (1996) A Historical and Contemporary Outline. London: Hodder and Stoughton.

Appadorai, M. A. (1975). *The Substance of Politics*, Ibadan: Oxford University Press

Arokodare, J. B. (1995). Political Economic System in Historical Perspective. In Olutimehin, J. T. B. and Dada, S. A. (eds) Essentials of General Studies. Ekiti: Petoa Educational Publishers

Ashcraft (1973), In Omolade, Z. A. and Adebamowo O. (eds) General Studies in Education, Ijebu-Ode: Dapo Educational Publishers

Asoga-Allen, K. O. (1998) The Relevance of Citizenship Education to National Development. In the proceedings of the National Colloquium on the Future of Primary Education in Nigeria. LACOPED - Noforija.

Asoga-Allen, K. O. (2000) Nigerian Society and Citizenship Education. *Journal of the Institute of Education* LASUJES Vol. 2.

Asoga-Allen, K. O. (2000) Nigerian Traditional Education and Western Education; The Effect of

Western Education on Nigerian Culture. In the Book of Readings on Students Unionism in Nigeria. A Cost Analysis of Effects (1970 - 2000) Noforija: LACOPED

Baskin, C. (2003) Structural Social Work as Seen From an Aboriginal Perspective in W. Shera (Ed.) Emerging Perspectives on anti Oppressive Practice (pp 65 - 78). Toronto: Canadian Scholar's Press.

Bhagwat (1996). In Omolade, Z. A. and Adebamowo O. (eds) General Studies in Education, Ijebu-Ode: Dapo Educational Publishers

Ekemode, K. O.; Arabami, O. A. and Sanbe, M. T. (2000) Agriculture and the Nigerian Economy, in Ekemode K. O. (ed.) Introduction to Agriculture for Sustainable Development. Lagos: National Association of Agricultural Educators (NAAGRED).

Ekuigbo, K. U. E. and Arokodare, J. B. (1995). Scientific Development in Nigeria, In Olutimehin J. T. B. and Dada, S. A. (eds), *Essentials of General Studies for Schools and Colleges*, Ado-Ekiti: Petoa Educational Publishers.

Ezewu, E. E. (1981) Education During the Middle

Ages, unpublished Mimeo, Faculty of Education, University of Ibadan.

Federal Ministry of Information (1986). *National Policy on Science and Technology*. Ibadan: Nihort Press.

Ijaduola, K. O. (1996). "Science and Society". In Omolade, Z. A. and Adebamowo O. (eds) General Studies in Education. Ijebu-Ode: Dapo Educational Publishers.

Kluchholn, C. (1951). The Concept of Culture in Learner D. and Lasswell, H. D. (eds). The Policy Sciences. Stanford: Standard University Press.

Leslie, D. R.; Leslie, K. & Murphy, M. (2003) Inclusion by Design: The Challenge for Social Work in Work Place Accommodation for People With Disabilities in W. Shera (Eds.) Emerging Perspective on Anti-Oppression Practice (pp. 157 - 169). Toronto: Canadian Scholar's Press

Lessa, I. (2006) Discursive Struggles Within Social Welfare: Restaging Teen Motherhood. British Journal of Social Work 36, 283 - 298

Linton, R. (1995) Present World Conditions in Culture Perspective, In Linton, R. (ed). The Science of

Man in World Crises: New York.

Moursund, D. (1992) Teachers Guide to Computers in Elementary School: Denver: Love Publishing Company.

Mullaly, B. (2000) Oppression: The Focus of Structural Social Work, in B. Mullay. The New Structural Social Work (pp. 252 - 286) Don Mills Oxford University Press.

Onimode B. (1993), In Omolade, Z. A. and Adebamowo O. (eds). *General Studies in Education*, Ijebu-Ode: Dapo Educational Publishers

Strivatsina (1975). In Omolade, Z. A. and Adebamowo, O. (eds) *General Studies in Education*, Ijebu-Ode: Dapo Educational Publishers

United Nations Education and Scientific Cooperation (UNESCO) (1979) *An Introduction to Policy Analysis in Science and Technology:* PARIS: UNESCO.

Young, I. M. (2000) Five Faces of Oppression. In M. Adams (Ed.) Readings for Diversity and Social Work (pp. 35 - 49). New York: Routledge

Index

A

B

C

www.ingramcontent.com/pod-product-compliance
Lightning Source LLC
Chambersburg PA
CBHW071400280526
45787CB00001B/392